New Directions for
Community Colleges

Arthur M. Cohen
EDITOR-IN-CHIEF

Caroline Q. Durdella
Nathan R. Durdella
ASSOCIATE EDITORS

Amy Fara Edwards
MANAGING EDITOR

Understanding Equity in Community College Practice

Erin L. Castro

EDITOR

Number 172 • Winter 2015
Jossey-Bass
San Francisco

UNDERSTANDING EQUITY IN COMMUNITY COLLEGE PRACTICE
Erin L. Castro (ed.)
New Directions for Community Colleges, no. 172

Arthur M. Cohen, Editor-in-Chief
Caroline Q. Durdella, Nathan R. Durdella, Associate Editors
Amy Fara Edwards, Managing Editor

NEW DIRECTIONS FOR COMMUNITY COLLEGES (ISSN 0194-3081, electronic ISSN 1536-0733) is part of The Jossey-Bass Higher and Adult Education Series and is published quarterly by Wiley Subscription Services, Inc., A Wiley Company, at Jossey-Bass, One Montgomery St., Ste. 1200, San Francisco, CA 94104. POSTMASTER: Send address changes to New Directions for Community Colleges, Jossey-Bass, One Montgomery St., Ste. 1200, San Francisco, CA 94104.

SUBSCRIPTIONS cost $89 for individuals in the U.S., Canada, and Mexico, and $113 in the rest of the world for print only; $89 in all regions for electronic only; $98 in the U.S., Canada, and Mexico for combined print and electronic; $122 for combined print and electronic in the rest of the world. Institutional print only subscriptions are $335 in the U.S., $375 in Canada and Mexico, and $409 in the rest of the world; electronic only subscriptions are $335 in all regions; combined print and electronic subscriptions are $402 in the U.S., $442 in Canada and Mexico, and $476 in the rest of the world.

Cover design: Wiley
Cover Images: © Lava 4 images | Shutterstock

EDITORIAL CORRESPONDENCE should be sent to the Editor-in-Chief, Arthur M. Cohen, at 1749 Mandeville Lane, Los Angeles, CA 90049. All manuscripts receive anonymous reviews by external referees.

New Directions for Community Colleges is indexed in CIJE: Current Index to Journals in Education (ERIC), Contents Pages in Education (T&F), Current Abstracts (EBSCO), Ed/Net (Simpson Communications), Education Index/Abstracts (H. W. Wilson), Educational Research Abstracts Online (T&F), ERIC Database (Education Resources Information Center), and Resources in Education (ERIC).

Microfilm copies of issues and articles are available in 16mm and 35mm, as well as microfiche in 105mm, through University Microfilms Inc., 300 North Zeeb Road, Ann Arbor, MI 48106-1346.

Contents

EDITOR'S NOTES   1
Erin L. Castro

1. Addressing the Conceptual Challenges of Equity Work: A   5
Blueprint for Getting Started
Erin L. Castro
This chapter provides an introduction to and description of educa-
tional equity. It outlines common traps to avoid when engaging equity-
oriented practices in community college contexts.

2. Why Diversity and Equity Matter: Reflections from a   15
Community College President
Francisco C. Rodriguez
What roles can leaders play to create, nurture, and sustain a campus
culture that supports equity? This chapter offers the candid views and
suggestions of an accidental leader, who now leads one of the largest
community college districts in the nation.

3. Developing Agency for Equity-Minded Change   25
Eric R. Felix, Estela Mara Bensimon, Debbie Hanson, James Gray,
Libby Klingsmith
This chapter highlights the use of the Equity Scorecard, a theory-based
strategy that assists community colleges in embedding equity into
their institutional norms, practices, and policies, with the Community
College of Aurora.

4. Pathways to Results: How Practitioners Address Student   43
Access, Outcomes, and Equity in an Associate Degree Nursing
Program
Jessica Pickel, Debra D. Bragg
Pathways to Results (PTR) engages practitioners in using data to close
equity gaps for student groups historically underserved by postsecondary education. This chapter describes the experiences of practitioners at Richland Community College who implemented PTR to improve
student access, outcomes, and equity in an associate degree nursing
program.

5. Call to Action: Embracing an Inclusive LGBTQ Culture on   57
Community College Campuses
Jason L. Taylor
Many community colleges are unwelcoming to LGBTQ students and
this chapter provides practical suggestions to community college lead-
ers to develop a more inclusive campus culture.

6. Do Financial Aid Policies Unintentionally Punish the Poor,   67
and What Can We Do About It?
Courtney A. Campbell, Regina Deil-Amen, Cecilia Rios-Aguilar
This chapter argues that, despite intentions, the ways that federal
financial aid policy is constructed and currently administered can have
negative consequences for poor community college students.

7. Salt Lake Community College Veterans Services: A Model of   77
Serving Veterans in Higher Education
Aaron Ahern, Michael Foster, Darlene Head
This chapter outlines the birth and growth of a veteran program in Salt
Lake City, Utah, and discuses next steps in spurring additional innova-
tions and advancements in better serving student veterans in commu-
nity colleges.

8. Undocumented Students at the Community College: 87
Creating Institutional Capacity
Jéssica I. Valenzuela, William Perez, Iliana Perez, Gloria Itzel Montiel,
Gabriel Chaparro
This chapter introduces Institutional Undocu-Competence (IUC), an
institutional capacity framework emerging from a critical analysis of
cultural competence, aimed to inform community colleges' efforts to
better support the growing undocumented student population.

9. Black Men Attending Community Colleges: Examining an   97
Institutional Approach Toward Equity
Lorenzo Baber, Randy Fletcher, Edmund Graham
This chapter outlines an institutional approach for improving condi-
tions for Black men on campus through an illustrative example of the
Together We Achieve program at Parkland College in Illinois.

INDEX   109

EDITOR'S NOTES

Institutional commitments to serving underrepresented student communities are now commonplace rhetoric, omnipresent across university mission statements and reflected in language such as access, opportunity, and inclusion. Perhaps this emphasis is nowhere more potent than in the community college sector, where 2-year institutions are routinely heralded as critical to serving a growing number of diverse student learners. The overarching theme evident in expressed commitments and language around equity is that institutions value diversity: differences in perspectives, people, and ideas. A commitment to ensuring that underrepresented student populations have access to the institution and are successful once enrolled is a growing concern among higher education leaders.

This volume is born of that concern and inspired by the following question: What do equity-oriented practices look like in different community college contexts? Given the current landscape of higher education and the increasing role of the community college in realizing equitable outcomes for students, examples of what practitioners are doing to move forward an equity agenda are urgently needed. Crucial to realizing the larger national goal of increasing outcomes for all groups of students, and particularly those who continue to be underserved by educational institutions, is an understanding of promising practices, perspectives, and experiences. The collection of diverse perspectives and issues contained within this volume aims to advance an equity agenda.

An abundance of literature and research exists documenting the inequitable educational experiences faced by underserved and underrepresented students in higher education. We know, for example, that students of Color and lower income students continue to be overrepresented in remedial and developmental education. We know that women remain vastly underrepresented in traditional male-dominated fields such as science, technology, engineering, and math (STEM). We know that by almost every higher education benchmark available, including graduation rate, time to degree, and transfer status, underserved students remain at a great disadvantage. We also know that an overwhelming majority of these students, including students of Color; first generation students; lower income students; undocumented students; lesbian, gay, bisexual, transgender, and/or queer (LGBTQ+)[1]; incarcerated and formerly incarcerated students; students with disabilities; English language learners; students who are veterans; refugee students; and other underserved populations, will attend or are currently attending community colleges. This volume uses the aforementioned research as a platform to show what community college practitioners are doing within these conditions; that is, we provide examples of how our understandings and practices within community college contexts are shifting to consider the larger sociostructural contours of inequity.

Collectively, the chapters in this volume provide practitioners with concrete examples of policy, programming, and thinking that emphasize the role of the community college in expanding educational opportunity for students amid the constraints posed by structural design: poverty, racism, and inadequate access to health care, among other systemic challenges. Driven by a change in thinking and imagination, these examples show how practitioners can—and should—tailor programming in light of larger patterns of inequality. It is my hope that in providing snapshots of how others are engaging this work, the following chapters promote conversations among practitioners about what equity means in tandem with what is considered fair in respective community college contexts.

Chapter 1 provides an introduction to and explanation of educational equity. It serves as a conceptual and practical foundation for the volume. In Chapter 2, Francisco C. Rodriguez explains why diversity and equity are important from the perspective of a community college president. Rodriguez currently leads one of the largest community college districts in the nation and in this chapter he offers candid views and suggestions on how upper-level leaders can promote and sustain a culture of educational equity.

Chapter 3, written by Eric R. Felix, Estela Mara Bensimon, Debbie Hanson, James Gray, and Libby Klingsmith, highlights the use of the Equity Scorecard, a theory-based strategy that assists community colleges in embedding equity into their institutional norms, practices, and policies, with the Community College of Aurora. Their chapter provides a much-needed example of decision making that is informed by strategic data collection and the development of institutional capacity. The following chapter, Chapter 4, extends the tenor of the previous one by turning to Pathways to Results (PTR), a problem-solving methodology developed by the Office of Community College Research and Leadership at the University of Illinois. Emphasizing equitable outcomes for students, Jessica Pickel and Debra D. Bragg highlight the use of PTR at Richland Community College in order to improve equity in an associate degree nursing program.

Chapter 5, written by Jason L. Taylor, focuses on the creation of an inclusive LGBTQ+ culture for community college campuses. Emphasizing the role of heterosexism and homophobia, Taylor shows why it is imperative for community colleges to be proactive in serving students who may identify as part of the LGBTQ+ community, and how practitioners can begin to challenge institutional norms that create inequitable experiences for LGBTQ+ students. Chapter 6 provides a critical analysis of financial aid policies and practices that may unintentionally discriminate against lower income students of Color. Written by Courtney A. Campbell, Regina Deil-Amen, and Cecilia Rios-Aguilar, this chapter exposes some of the consequences of financial aid policies for lower income students and provides practitioners with recommendations in correcting contemporary approaches to disbursement.

Chapter 7, written by Aaron Ahern, Michael Foster, and Darlene Head, highlights the Veterans Service Center at Salt Lake Community College. Recognized as one of *Military Times'* "Best for Vets" community colleges in the country, Salt Lake Community College ranked number 11 in 2014. In this chapter the authors outline some of the thinking and planning that went into creating their center and establishing critical partnerships with community agencies. Chapter 8, written by Jéssica I. Valenzuela, William Perez, Iliana Perez, Gloria Itzel Montiel, and Gabriel Chaparro, focuses on creating equity for a growing number of community college students who are undocumented. Serving students who are undocumented presents a number of challenges; using as a framework of Institutional Undocu-Competence (IUC), the authors provide practitioners with information on how to begin to create institutional capacity for equitably serving undocumented students.

In Chapter 9, Lorenzo Baber, Randy Fletcher, and Edmund Graham examine an institutional approach toward achieving equity for Black men attending community colleges. Through an illustrative example of a program at Parkland College in Illinois, their chapter provides information and recommendations for improving the conditions and climate for Black men on community college campuses.

To be certain, there are gaps in this collection. There are many more chapters that I would have liked to include but simply could not because of space restrictions. This volume also emphasizes student-level equity, which is only one angle of institutional equity. It is my hope that this special edition is the first of many in the future dedicated to educational equity and practice. Future volumes on equity could examine institutional elements of equity, such as faculty, staff, administration, and curriculum, as well as other important components of equity-oriented practices in community college contexts.

Finally, I am compelled to share that I am very proud of this volume of *New Directions for Community Colleges.* It has been an honor to work with a collection of committed authors—researchers, community college leaders and practitioners, activists and advocates—who are unabashedly moving forward an equity agenda, even amid obstacles and environmental constraints. Finding the time to write and doing so in the spirit of educating others is a wonderful example of praxis, an example of generosity that we will need in order to actualize more equitable educational institutions and experiences for all students.

Note

1. LGBTQ+ is used throughout the volume to be inclusive of all individuals who wish to identify with this community.

Erin L. Castro
Editor

ERIN L. CASTRO *is an assistant professor in the Department of Educational Leadership and Policy at the University of Utah.*

NEW DIRECTIONS FOR COMMUNITY COLLEGES • DOI: 10.1002/cc

1

This chapter provides an introduction to and description of educational equity. It outlines common traps to avoid when engaging equity-oriented practices in community college contexts.

Addressing the Conceptual Challenges of Equity Work: A Blueprint for Getting Started

Erin L. Castro

What is equity? I want to begin this chapter by asking what it means to think about equity in a particularly difficult social moment, one of widening economic inequality and social fracture. A seemingly obvious question, but perhaps this is why it begs further attention. Many of us routinely use the word equity, participate in and facilitate programs that aim to increase equity, and work for institutions that espouse commitments to equity. But what does equity really mean? And, conversely, what might it mean to think about equity? I am interested in how we think about equity and how this thinking influences practice: how it influences our perceptions of students, our interactions with students, and the programs we design to help facilitate their success.

Although it is rather easy to agree with broad rhetorical commitments to a more just and equitable society, the barriers to *practicing* equity are many. In fact, equity-oriented practices are difficult to engage because of a complex system of sociopolitical and economic relations. Thus, walking the walk, so to speak, requires a thoughtful understanding of how community colleges are situated within a larger social landscape and accordingly, how community college practice affects the scope of opportunities made available to students on campus. In their latest book, Dowd and Bensimon (2015) contend that equity can be thought of as a standard. Equity as a standard can then be used in community college practice to judge "whether a state of affairs is just or unjust" (p. 9). Thinking about equity as a standard is useful because it surfaces important considerations related to ideas of fairness. What do we believe that people deserve, and why? In the context of community college practice, what do we believe that our students deserve, and why?

New Directions for Community Colleges, no. 172, Winter 2015 © 2015 Wiley Periodicals, Inc.
Published online in Wiley Online Library (wileyonlinelibrary.com) • DOI: 10.1002/cc.20159

5

Although our individual answers may slightly differ, I believe that we all want students to be successful and we want them to be provided with the tools and resources to thrive. We know, however, that not all students—or potential students—are provided with what they need in order to realize their full potential and this is really at the heart of equity. What I'd like to propose in this first chapter is that it is not only important for us to design programming around equity but also to think deeply about what equity means, what it might look like, and what it might feel like on community college campuses. Practice is greatly influenced by the way we think about equity and what we think equity means. Because equity is a contextually dependent construct, how we consider that context—that is, where we decide to look and what we decide to see—greatly matters. In fact, I might go so far as to say that vision is the most important element of engaging equity-oriented practice: to see our current circumstances for what they are and then to envision a reality-based path toward equitable change. Accordingly, my purpose in this chapter is to focus on vision and in so doing, encourage a rethinking of commonplace approaches, attitudes, and assumptions toward persistent challenges of disparity in community college spaces and to outline common pitfalls in attempting equity work.

What Is Equity (and What Is It Not)?

Popular rhetoric around difference in U.S. higher education routinely includes buzzwords such as "diversity" and "inclusion," but these terms are not synonymous with equity. Issues of diversity and inclusion are important concepts to understand, to be certain, but they are not the same thing as understanding equity. To understand equity is to understand power and the ways in which power operates throughout society.

Power may feel like an intimidating subject, but it need not be. Understanding power is really about seeing how privilege and disadvantage operate throughout society and, therefore, how these operations affect individuals and groups of people over time. Concepts like privilege and disadvantage emphasize structural and institutional patterns that, when examined from a macro level, position individuals and groups of people in particular advantageous and/or disadvantageous ways throughout society. In the context of community college practice, privilege and disadvantage can be seen in the ways that students interact with and are positioned by the resources made available to them: financial aid policies, academic advising practices, student support services, and everyday interactions with college administrators, faculty, and staff, among other resources.

Plainly stated, equity in higher education is the idea that students from historically and contemporarily marginalized and minoritized communities have access to what they need in order to be successful. This is not a radical proposition and in the abstract, it is probably something with which we can all agree. Providing students with what they need in order to be successful is not simply reasonable, it's our job. However, understanding equity as a function of power can quickly become complicated; what if we aren't quite sure what students need? How do we know if we are adequately providing students with what they need? Because some students' needs are different from others', is it fair to give different kinds of resources to different groups of students?

The answers to these questions are varied, but asking them is an important step in the process of engaging equity-oriented practices in community colleges. The unfortunate reality is that we do not spend enough time asking these kinds of questions and as a result, we may not have the opportunity to think deeply about how to achieve equity. Accordingly, our attempts to appropriately address disparities in student access, experience, and outcomes may be misguided.

Because equity is about power, to engage equity-oriented practices in community college contexts means to work toward changing powerful systems: systemic practices, regulations, norms, and habits of the institution. This is difficult work, at least in part, because it can be hard for the individuals performing habits and norms to see them. In order for policy and programming to be equity oriented, they need to be aimed at transforming permanent institutional assumptions and practices that privilege some student groups and not others. An emphasis on diversity or inclusion falls short of this aim.

Commitments to diversity or inclusion do not require a critical attention to power in the same way as equity. For example, we can appeal to notions of diversity and never disrupt the practices that make it difficult for lower income students to persist. Or, we can commit to notions of inclusivity without ever addressing hostile campus climates for students of Color. Or, we can celebrate difference through ceremonial gatherings and special weeks dedicated to disenfranchised groups without adequately addressing deeply held assumptions about particular student communities, including undocumented students; lesbian, gay, bisexual, transgender, and/or queer (LGBTQ+) students; or pregnant and parenting students; among others. Certainly, these kinds of events serve a purpose on campus and I am not arguing that we need to eliminate them, but we need to recognize them for what they are and what they do, as well as where they fall short.

I would like for us to move us away from ideas of diversity and inclusion, not because they do not matter, but because they are simply not enough to address entrenched disparity in higher education. We need a politics of equity in community college practice that moves beyond simply increasing numerical representation of underrepresented groups or celebrating difference, because the mere presence of difference does not equal equity. Normative structural and institutional patterns that place underrepresented students in disadvantaged positions must be addressed, and the only way to do this is to see them for what they are and understand how they operate. Certainly numerical representation is one aspect of this work, but creating the capacity to successfully and humanely serve and support growing numbers of underrepresented students should be the ultimate institutional goal.

Challenges in Doing Equity Work

There are a number of challenges in transforming community college spaces to become more equitable. In what follows, I focus on three broad challenges that are common throughout higher education in general, as well as community college practice. My fundamental assumption in providing the following challenges is that equity is about power. Many of the following examples may alleviate short-term issues; however, they collectively neglect to address structural conditions that perpetuate inequity. The following dispositions all function to alleviate the immediate, which is surely an important component of working toward equity but not enough to engage transformational change. Falling into any of the following thinking patterns ultimately works to sustain inequity in the long term because the following habits do not disrupt the root causes of inequity: unfair distributions of power.

Focusing on the Student Instead of the Institution.   Throughout higher education there exists a commonsensical culture as it relates to addressing disparity. If a group of students is not performing well in developmental reading courses, for example, the popular response is to target individual students for academic intervention programming. If women are underrepresented in advanced math courses, the likely response is to recruit more women into such programs. Likewise, if African-American students are not persisting and completing at the same rates as their White peers, then a program is typically designed to assist individual African-American students in completing. The institutional responses to student failure rates, issues of racialized academic achievement, or gendered representation overwhelmingly privilege intervention programming aimed at assisting individual students.

Although targeting individual student communities is perhaps one component of working toward equity, doing so is only a partial fix to a more complex problem. It makes sense to target individual student communities only if individual students are the problem. What I've tried to point out thus far is that individual student communities are not the problem, but rather the way we tend to think about equity is the problem. As practitioners, we need to look in different directions in order to see more complex problems and imagine more appropriate solutions. In essence, we need to relearn where to look and what to see.

Because intervention programs aimed at individuals tend only to scratch the surface of the deeper work that needs to be done, important examinations of institutional thinking and practice may not occur. Programs that target individual students can be thought of as surface-level programming because they do not interrupt more permanent institutional practices. In fact, surface-level programming may *assist* in the maintenance of inequitable structures because such programming fails to disrupt normative routines and processes that perpetually position individual students as "in need" of assistance. The important point of consideration here is this: who is being blamed for educational neglect (popularly known as "underpreparation") and consequently targeted for intervention programming? If individual students rather than institutional structures (e.g., policies, practices, and people) are the focus, then even well-intended intervention programming may contribute to the maintenance of inequity.

Thinking About Students From a Deficit Perspective.   One of the most common ways that underrepresented students are conceptualized in postsecondary education is through a deficit lens. There is a deeply rooted history in the United States related to deficit framing of underrepresented students in higher education, particularly students of Color, women, and lower income students. Valencia (2010) refers to the practice of deficit framing in education as educational deficit thinking, which has negative consequences for students and is incongruent with equity-oriented practices.

Educational deficit thinking occurs when institutions, through their policies, practices, language, and thinking, blame individual students for what they perceivably lack. Popular examples include referring to students as "at risk" for failure or labeling students as "underprepared" (Castro, 2014). The problem with locating failure within individual students is that it lets off the hook other institutional and systemic factors such as inadequate programming at the postsecondary level, underresourced secondary schools, and underdeveloped viable career pathways. When individual students are blamed for not having access to academic preparedness and then consequently targeted for intervention programming in college, they become problems to be fixed.

The error in this perspective is that it fails to account for *why* students may arrive on community college campuses with disparate access to sufficient academic preparation. Without attention toward the structural conditions that position students in disadvantaged ways, programming will always be necessary to assist individual students because it is not aimed at challenging the conditions that contribute to their disadvantage. Programs that exist to assist academically "underprepared" students or those who are "at risk" for failure make explicit the goals of the program: change the student to align with the standards of the institution. Certainly, we want students academically proficient and positioned to perform well academically, but intervention programs that are designed to target students' labeled deficiencies are limited in their ability to turn around and ask the same questions of the institution: How and in what ways is the institution underprepared to successfully serve students? In what ways is the institution "at risk" for failing students?

NEW DIRECTIONS FOR COMMUNITY COLLEGES • DOI: 10.1002/cc

Neglecting Institutional Climate.   A consequence of the previous two challenges is that the institutional environment is neglected when energy is narrowly targeted toward individual students. It is important to think about the larger campus environment into which underrepresented and underserved students are recruited, and this includes both the academic and social spaces that they will navigate. Campus climate (Hurtado, 1992; Hurtado & Ruiz, 2012) is a useful construct to consider when thinking about equity.

Campus climate brings together the social and institutional contexts that affect the ways that students experience colleges and universities. Oftentimes, colleges are unaware of how underrepresented students experience campus and collegiate environments. As a result, well-intended practitioners may be recruiting underrepresented students into hostile or unhealthy environments where students encounter bias, discrimination, and/or feelings of exclusion. It is important to consider how underrepresented students may experience the institution as members of a minoritized group. Students interact with a number of individuals who work for the institution through normative processes, such as registering for classes, meeting with an advisor, attending classes, and interacting in social spaces. It is the responsibility of the institution to ensure that the individuals representing the college are committed to equity and that routine practices—including habits, dispositions, norms, and regulations—reflect this commitment.

Focusing on equitable student outcomes (see Felix et al., Chapter 3) requires that practitioners are attentive to the environment into which they are welcoming underrepresented and traditionally undervalued student communities. Increasing equitable outcomes for students means that we also want to know about students' experiences and interactions with faculty, staff, administrators, and peers on campus or in an online classroom environment. Faculty, staff, and administrators need continual education and new knowledge to help support the success of students who may experience the world and the institution differently than they do. As Rodriguez points out in this volume, practitioners need to know that equity is an institutional value and they should be given the knowledge and resources to work toward this goal. Understanding how underrepresented students experience the climate of the institution is an important place to begin this work.

Relearning Where to Look and What to See

> There can never be a single story, there are only ways of seeing.
> Arundhati Roy (2002)

The challenges described here stem from a commonsensical and historically rooted culture in higher education as it relates to widening access for traditionally excluded communities. Although popular, these approaches are ineffective in addressing disparity in the long term. Part of our responsibility as practitioners, educators, and scholars is to recognize the work we need to do in order to transform institutions into spaces committed to equity. As I mentioned previously, this work begins by the way that we see things: where we choose to look and what we choose to see.

Felix et al. and Pickel and Bragg (this volume) each provide examples of shifting practitioners' gaze and questioning problematic assumptions. They provide examples and concrete tools to use in working through familiar ways of looking at problems toward more imaginative and bold approaches to justice. At the heart of their suggestions lie useful questions that can help in relearning where to look and avoiding some of the common thinking traps of doing equity work: Are individual students being blamed? Are problems being identified before knowing all of the information? Are issues of institutional climate being considered? These types of questions effectively remove the emphasis of equity away from an individual frame and position it as an institutional one, a key component of engaging equity work.

In the introduction I asked what it might mean to think about equity because thinking about equity beyond program design should push us to (re)consider practice. We may be encouraged to recognize how we see the world and, perhaps, to think about how others might see it, too. At the very least, I believe thinking about equity encourages us to examine concepts like privilege and disadvantage and why some individuals have access to opportunities and others do not. Reflecting upon these questions is the necessary groundwork for equity-oriented practices.

When we desire a more fair and balanced society, one where resources are more equitably distributed and accessible to those with the least economic and political power, we appeal to a fundamental ideal: justice. When we imagine what it might be like to walk in someone else's shoes—to perhaps experience life in unfamiliar ways, we humanize the sociopolitical conditions that comprise the status quo, the very conditions to which we have become so accustomed, such as gross educational inequity along the lines of race and class throughout all levels of education.

Systemic structures, such as entrenched poverty or inequality of educational opportunity, are not insurmountable, but we must see them for what they are and recognize that they need not be permanent fixtures of our society. They can be transformed and community colleges play a crucial role in this transformation. But, because inequity quite literally surrounds us, working for a more just society can be an arduous undertaking. It is easy to become jaded or feel that what we do in everyday practice cannot possibly make a difference.

New Directions for Community Colleges • DOI: 10.1002/cc

But it does.

Certainly, we cannot engage mass change overnight. But, we can do small things with conviction that ultimately make a difference at our respective institutions. This work can begin by recognizing how we see our students and their circumstances and asking, quite frankly, what we think they deserve.

Conclusion

We do not exist independently from one another, even if our world is organized in ways to make us believe otherwise. Once we accept this fact, we can engage our work with students with compassion instead of pity and understanding instead of judgment. We can see that we are not able to fix everything, but that we can work across coalitions of difference and use the power we do have to create change. As educators and practitioners, we must see ourselves as part of a larger picture and recognize that what we choose to do at our respective institutions is just as important as what we choose *not* to do. Our work matters not simply for those student communities who we want to assist in being successful but for all of us.

We must locate our work somewhere along the spectrum, where students have the individual agency to overcome great odds and where we, as equity-oriented practitioners, recognize and work against the very real structural obstacles that stand in their way. We need a more meaningful, long-lasting solution to systemic inequity in community college spaces, one that recognizes that the success of any equity-oriented program should ultimately be its own abolishment. The fact that we continue to need programming aimed at increasing equity means that we still have a lot of work to do.

I am inspired by the idea that a more fair and just world is possible. By positioning equity as a function of power, we can better see the origins of systemic inequity and understand their durability. We can then design more effective programming that gets at the source of the problem, not simply its all-too-familiar symptoms.

References

Castro, E. L. (2014). "Underprepared" and "at-risk": Disrupting deficit discourses in undergraduate STEM recruitment and retention programming. *Journal of Student Affairs Research and Practice, 51*(4), 407–419.

Dowd, A., & Bensimon, E. (2015). *Engaging the "race question": Accountability and equity in U.S. higher education.* New York: Teachers College Press.

Hurtado, S. (1992). The campus racial climate: Contexts of conflict. *The Journal of Higher Education, 63*(5), 539–569.

Hurtado, S., & Ruiz, A. (2012). *The climate for underrepresented groups and diversity on campus* (Research Brief). Los Angeles: Higher Education Research Institute at UCLA. Retrieved from http://www.heri.ucla.edu/briefs/urmbriefreport.pdf

Roy, A. (2002). *Come September*. Lecture conducted from Santa Fe, NM.

Valencia, R. (2010). *Dismantling contemporary deficit thinking: Educational thought and practice*. New York, NY: Routledge.

ERIN L. CASTRO is an assistant professor in the Department of Educational Leadership and Policy at the University of Utah.

2

What roles can leaders play to create, nurture, and sustain a campus culture that can ultimately lead to improving student success, to diversifying the ranks of faculty and administrators, and to facilitating meaningful engagement concerning the critical issues of diversity, equity, and inclusion? This chapter offers the candid views and suggestions of an accidental leader, who now leads one of the largest community college districts in the nation.

Why Diversity and Equity Matter: Reflections from a Community College President

Francisco C. Rodriguez

Introduction

Why do the issues of diversity and equity have such resonance for me? As a first-generation immigrant, English-language learner from a working-class family, access to higher education and the opportunity that followed was the door to personal discovery and professional exploration, a door to a renewed hope that was counter to the generations of poverty and isolation that my family and my ancestors had endured, unselfishly, all for the chance that the next generation would be better off than the one before.

I am in my 30th year of service to public higher education and now find myself chancellor of the Los Angeles Community College District (LACCD), a constellation of nine accredited colleges serving over 150,000 students each semester. In coming to Los Angeles, I feel like I am coming back home to San Francisco. The noise, the smells, the sounds, the whole urban vibe speaks to me and I am very comfortable in it. I know and possess urban sensibilities and they have served me well in my transition. My principal goal is to raise the educational attainment of our students while ensuring that our colleges, spread throughout this large district, represent the communities they serve.

Like so many other urban community colleges, LACCD is riddled with challenges and opportunities. In fact, over 80% of entering students are not considered college ready by national benchmarks, requiring that they enroll in remedial coursework. If you disaggregate the data by gender,

New Directions for Community Colleges, no. 172, Winter 2015 © 2015 Wiley Periodicals, Inc.
Published online in Wiley Online Library (wileyonlinelibrary.com) • DOI: 10.1002/cc.20160

ethnicity, neighborhoods, socioeconomic status, and zip code, this disparity and inequity are exacerbated. More than 50% of the students enrolled each semester live at or below the poverty line, 85% of them come from traditionally underserved and underrepresented communities, and most are first-generation college attendees.

Some look at this position in this district, in this city and think, "Too large, too urban, too diverse, too poor, too many low scores on the student scorecard, too this, too that. I'll take a pass on the job." For me, those are exactly all the reasons why I said yes.

I am drawn to working in a large, urban district that desires to raise its educational profile and leverage its size to help the working-class and low-income students get the support they need to be successful. To be a leader in such a diverse district is very attractive, as I, like so many of my community college colleagues, am committed to the common and public good. It reminds me of the horrible attacks of 9/11 in 2001 when brave, selfless first responders and firefighters were running into buildings about to collapse—what remarkable, inspiring courage and profound sense of duty. Our public education system needs people as educators running into, not out of, these districts that could stand to be improved. And I am proud to be a part of that.

Like so many of our students, my parents came to this country with little formal education, yet they held onto the dreams and aspirations of their children with a firm grip. At an early age, this became very apparent to me as I observed and listened, sometimes with dismay, but more often with amazement and joy, to the conversations that took place around the kitchen table of my childhood home in the Mission District of San Francisco. It was an ordinary kitchen table, with six chairs, but it holds a special significance to me for a variety of reasons. For this was the table where our family gathered to eat my mother's savory dishes, to learn of local happenings and world events, and to hear the stories of struggle and of resilience that my family or my extended family was undergoing in adjusting to life in this country as "foreigners." I often looked over to my parents and saw the vestiges of hard work and a tireless work ethic exemplified: their dark, tired eyes; my father's thick, bronze hands compliments of the cannery where he worked for more than 30 years; my mother's swollen ankles, a constant reminder of her 30-year post in an industrial laundry factory, where she stood all day and washed and pressed the linens of our city's best restaurants.

The kitchen table was also the place where I learned of and became exposed to the hurtful themes and practice of bias, discrimination, and prejudice. And because there was no desk and lamp at our home, the kitchen table was also the place where we all did our homework and school projects; it is the place where I discovered my zeal for learning and my passion for public service.

As I matured and transitioned from my boyhood table to high school college-prep courses and university life, I became conscious that I was a direct beneficiary of programs and funding designed to attract, enroll, and serve historically underrepresented populations in higher education. I felt and in many ways still feel a sense of indebtedness to those who came before me and bravely and unselfishly advocated to give people like me a chance, an opportunity—a hand up, not a handout. Yes, access and opportunity created through affirmative action, diversity, equity, and inclusion programs are the reasons that I am here today. As educators, I believe that it is our collective responsibility to purposefully serve our higher education community and, at the same time, to challenge it. We have perhaps the best opportunity to eradicate and overcome social and racial injustice and to empower the least educated and economically poorest in our communities. It is not just politically expedient or fiscally prudent to reach out and bring students in, especially those who have been historically underserved and underrepresented; it is simply and fundamentally the right thing to do.

The Time Is Now

The American community college system is the most egalitarian system of higher education in the world. We accept the top 100% of every high school graduating class, all of them without exception and without apology. We accept learners of all ages at any point in their life. Our colleges are beacons of hope and opportunity. For some, they are the first chance to go to college, and for others, the last and only chance.

An often misunderstood and forgotten branch of higher education, community colleges are receiving unprecedented national attention. The dialogue surrounding institutional performance and student success in the 2-year system is resounding. Virtually every community college in the country is focused on ways to improve success rates of all students, with special attention toward historically underperforming students, who now make up a growing proportion of student enrollments.

There is, however, cause for concern. At a time that President Barack Obama has challenged our community colleges to graduate an additional 5 million students by 2020 through the American Graduates Initiative, academic success realized by community college students is disproportionate by race, gender, and income among those who graduate. Multiple reports over the last 10 years also point to the societal impact of changing demographics, fueled by the highest immigration rates in nearly a century, and the skills gap that exists in literacy and numeracy needed for 21st century jobs in the knowledge-based economy. Many researchers and scholars have suggested that creating the conditions for better student performance outcomes in community college contexts will require a fundamental shift in culture and expectations. Therefore, in its broadest, nonpartisan context, our nation's strength, economic health and prosperity, and democracy depend on the inclusion and success of all its participants.

The role of community college leadership is imperative in bolstering institutional graduation rates and student learning outcomes that are equitable. College presidents must lead the dialogue on the issues of diversity, equity, and inclusion and, invariably, that will require justification for our efforts. We will need to address why equity matters and be specific about what can be done to create, nurture, and sustain a campus culture that can ultimately lead to improving student success, to diversifying the ranks of faculty and administrators, and to facilitating meaningful engagement concerning the critical issues of diversity and equity.

Why It Matters

During the civil rights era, persuasive arguments were made concerning the educational benefits of diversity and inclusion, which led to both federal and statewide legislation mandating a transparent process for folding in communities who had been historically and systematically marginalized from reaping the full benefits of our American democracy. The sanction for not complying with the law could lead to a loss of federal funding for publicly funded institutions. But perhaps the most dramatic example of my lifetime where a shift in the American consciousness occurred and the nation pivoted is Dr. Martin Luther King's iconic "I Have A Dream" speech, delivered powerfully on the steps of the Capitol Mall in 1963. Dr. King wielded his moral authority and used masterful oratory to convince a nation that equity and inclusion were necessary for our nation's democracy and societal well-being. Not long thereafter, the landmark federal Civil Rights Act and the Voting Rights Act were signed. Many of today's powerful institutions of inclusion and equity have their foundations in these laws and principles.

At the national level, contrary to popular belief, affirmative action programs still exist, notwithstanding the current state battles that question the necessity, soundness, and legality of affirmative action policies. There are legal safeguards that allow for diversity and equity efforts to continue and flourish. At the highest level, there are federal mandates and regulations, some through President Obama's Executive Orders, designed to ensure equal employment opportunity, including placement goals—not quotas—for hiring underrepresented groups.

American higher education is also speaking out. As one example, the Washington Higher Education Secretariat (WHES), formed in 1962, comprises chief executives from approximately 50 associations, each of which serves a significant sector or function in postsecondary education. In July 2013, WHES issued a statement printed in the *New York Times* that was signed by 37 higher education organizations reaffirming diversity in higher education as a national priority and underscoring the educational benefits of diversity and "the longstanding legal principle that the educational benefits of a widely student body are a compelling governmental interest" (WHES, 2013, para. 1). The statement goes on to proclaim, "We strongly agree and we remain dedicated to the mission of discovering and disseminating knowledge, including the knowledge gained through direct experiences with diverse colleagues—a resource for achieving stronger democracy in our nation" (para. 4).

Generally less visible and public is the discussion surrounding the paucity of faculty and administrators of Color in higher education and/or the tangible benefits of diverse teaching and leadership communities. This raises important questions about institutional climate, hiring practices, and equity on campus, to name a few. When these historically prickly issues are placed in the context of institutional tension caused by a protracted environment of constricted financial resources and "zero-sum" budgetary exercises, tensions can flare and cause healthy, constructive dialogue on diversity and equity issues to be marginalized, silenced, or dormant.

A Need for Leadership

A lack of consensus and leadership on issues of equity and diversity has affected the performance of underrepresented students, as their outcomes remain largely unchanged for 3 decades. Without another major shift in diversity, equity, and inclusion in higher education, our profession runs the risk of further bifurcation and passive perpetuation of racial inequality. This is the core finding of a study by the Georgetown University Center on Education and the Workforce (CEW), *Separate and Unequal: How Higher Education Reinforces the Intergenerational Reproduction of White Racial Privilege* (Carnevale & Strohl, 2013). The report contends that the higher education system is increasingly complicit as a passive agent in the systematic reproduction of White racial privilege across generations.

Jeff Strohl, one of the coauthors, states, "The American postsecondary system increasingly has become a dual system of racially separate pathways, even as overall minority access to the postsecondary system has grown dramatically" (para. 3). The authors find that White overrepresentation in the nation's most elite and competitive colleges (top 468 colleges) is increasing even as the White share of college-age students has declined. Among the findings:

- Since 1995, more than 80% of new White enrollments have been at the top 468 colleges and more than 70% of new African-American and Latino enrollments have been at the nation's open-access 2-year and 4-year colleges.
- Furthermore, as Whites are moving up into the top 468 colleges, they are vacating the open-access 2-year and 4-year colleges. Between 1995 and 2009 the White share of enrollments in open-access 2-year and 4-year colleges declined from 69% to 57%.

NEW DIRECTIONS FOR COMMUNITY COLLEGES • DOI: 10.1002/cc

According to a 2013 report by the Campaign for College Opportunity, a California advocacy group, more African-American students in California are earning bachelor's degrees than they were a decade ago, but enrollment in the state's public universities is stagnant and many are turning to costly for-profit schools. The report asserts that the road to graduation for Black students is still pitted with obstacles, despite efforts to close achievement gaps that have persisted over the years. Among the findings of this report:

- African-American students have the lowest completion rates for freshman and transfer students at all three higher education segments: community colleges, California State University, and the University of California (UC).
- African-American students are more likely than any other group to attend college without earning a degree.
- In 2012, more African-American students were enrolled at private, for-profit colleges than at California State University and UC combined.
- The achievement gap between African-Americans and Whites earning a bachelor's degree or higher has narrowed by only a percentage point over the last decade. In 2011, about 24% of African-American adults had obtained a bachelor's compared with 41% of Whites.

A 2013 report released by the same organization found similar hurdles in higher education for Latinos/as.

Resources Matter

I was talking to my son, Andres, about the educational achievement gap and he said, "Dad, it's not about achievement, it is about opportunity, because not everybody starts at the same place. So how can you expect the same outcomes to occur?" This is a wise observation from a young scholar. He's right—people do not all start at the same place. There is a disproportionate impact on access and outcomes for those who are poor, those who are first generation, and those who are known as linguistic minorities, among other underrepresented groups.

The lack of significant progress in diversity and equity is tied to funding because ultimately resources matter. The Georgetown University study (Carnevale & Strohl, 2013) that I previously cited indicates that the nation's selective colleges spend anywhere from two to almost five times as much on instruction per student as the open-access colleges, like community colleges. Even among equally qualified White, African-American, and Latino/a students, these pathways are not only separate but they bring unequal results:

- More than 30% of African-Americans and Hispanics with a high school grade point average (GPA) higher than 3.5 go to community colleges compared with 22% of Whites with the same GPA.
- Among students who score in the top half of test score distribution in the nation's high schools and attend college, 51% of White students get a bachelor's degree or higher compared with 34% of African-American students and 32% of Hispanic students.

One way to strengthen college pathways in the name of equity is to increase the amount of funding allocated toward supporting underrepresented and nontraditional student communities and nondominant completion pathways. In the current budget climate, this is a challenge. In California, for example, from 2009 to 2013, the public higher education budget that funds the University of California, California State University (CSU), and the California Community Colleges (CCC) was cut by $2.5 billion. The budgets for the state's 112 community college serving 2.6 million students were slashed by 12%, or $809 million, which translated to a loss of 485,000 students to the system during the same period. Tuition at UC and CSU nearly doubled during that time and the cost to enroll at a community college has increased by 77% in those years. Mercifully, the budget news was much better in 2014 for all segments of the state's public higher education system, fueled by a recovering economy and passage of Proposition 30 in 2012, a temporary tax initiative that funds schools and colleges.

The Role of the College President

To be successful, presidents must understand and in many ways reflect the mission, demographics, and culture of the institutions they lead. A recent report by The Aspen Institute and Achieving the Dream (2014) contends that presidents need to possess certain qualities, including a deep commitment to student access and success; a willingness to take significant risks to advance student success; an ability to create lasting change within the college; a broad strategic vision for the college and its students, reflected in external partnerships; and the ability to raise and allocate resources in ways aligned with student success. I wholeheartedly agree and would add an additional insight: As it relates to sustaining diversity and equity, institutional efforts must be aligned, intentional, and supported by a cross-section of the campus community and governing board. Leadership for these efforts must have a stalwart champion—the college president.

As an educator at the University of California, California State University, and California Community Colleges, 11 years as a community college president and now chancellor, I have witnessed the multiple and tangible benefits of having diverse faculty, administrators, and students of Color on campus, both to the institution and, more important, to the learning and engagement of students. Having administrators and faculty of Color that reflect the diversity of the students that we serve is not only beneficial to students of Color, but to the entire student body.

Several studies underscore the benefits of what I have observed. Administrators of Color serve as mentors for faculty of Color on campus and guide, said faculty who are considering the administrative pathway. Faculty of Color also serve as role models and mentors for students of Color (Gutierrez, Castañeda, & Katsinas, 2002) and provide encouragement for succeeding academically and facilitating their career aspirations (Cole & Barber, 2003). In 2001, the University of California President Richard Atkinson wrote to the nine chancellors of the system and stated that increasing faculty diversity is one of the valuable consequences of a commitment to a broad and diverse academic curriculum. "Continued academic excellence will require increased attention to issues such as multiculturalism, economic opportunity, and educational equity to ensure that they are reflected strongly in the University's teaching, curriculum, and research," he said (University of California, Office of the President, 2001, para. 1).

To promote institutional change on community college campuses, the "Three Cs" of Courage, Conviction, and *Coraje* (valor and boldness) are necessary. Courage refers to the courage to lead and to facilitate conversations, sometimes difficult ones, and to speak out for social justice and equity and get people to follow their convictions and to redress the disparities. This is important because leadership is not done by an individual but by a movement of change agents and by those committed to morally just causes. Conviction is the ability to stick to it for the long haul because change requires persistence. Best practices may not work right away and it may take a longer time to germinate into systems that allow for that to occur. *Coraje* is tied to the notion that things aren't right. It's not right that there are a disproportionate number of people who are poor and in prison and are low performing in our schools. To state it differently, it's simply unacceptable.

The role of the college president is to facilitate these courageous and difficult conversations about departmental expectations and institutional culture surrounding diversity, equity, and inclusion, especially related to hiring. With the number of faculty and administrators who are and will be going into retirement, there will be multiple job openings to fill. However, we cannot just expect excellent candidates to show up. Our institutions have to be intentional about whom we seek to bring into our academic community and be clear about the profile characteristics of the instructors and administrators we are looking for that would serve the institution well today and in the future. If we are committed to equity, it is necessary that we seek diversity among our faculty.

At the hiring table, I have heard it said, "Oh, we just don't have a diversified pool for a particular position." I believe the pool is often there, but qualified candidates may not always be advanced to the next level or ultimately selected. So, we need to ask why. I have seen colleges and departments looking for a replication of younger models of those to be replaced, perhaps those that we infer we will be more comfortable with, a profile or portrait that we recognize, instead of one that could be a stronger long-term asset. We need to look not at who the person is today, but who they can become with the support of the institution.

The college president has the responsibility of setting the tone for the organization. In my experience of recommending faculty and administrators for hire over the last 15 years, desirable candidates are also interviewing your campus and assessing whether this is a place for their professional and personal growth. Unlike other segments of higher education, community college faculty tend to retire from the institutions that first hire them. Top candidates want to know about the climate of the academic community they are potentially joining. Will I be supported and nurtured through the tenure and evaluation process? What are my departmental colleagues like? What are the opportunities for professional growth? What is the institutional commitment to diversity and inclusion issues? These are just some of the questions candidates ask, so paying attention to these questions can make the difference between attracting and hiring or losing top-flight candidates.

Conclusion

For community college educators, it is easy to see why higher education in general and community colleges in particular are such wonderful places in which to work. It is here where we can intertwine our professional craft as educators with our personal values. At the community colleges, we are proud of and reaffirm our values as open-access institutions whose hallmarks of affordability, accessibility, and outstanding quality are wrapped around an ethos of care and commitment—a commitment, in my view, to the goals of academic excellence, public service, diversity, and equity unparalleled in any segment of higher education.

College presidents can't do this work alone. Part of our role is to create a community of like-minded individuals who support excellence in diversity, equity, and inclusion efforts. Part of this job is to create a climate of inclusion and trust and to empower and support others who are positioned to make these changes.

As educators we must cross boundaries and solve the vexing issues surrounding student success in an interdisciplinary fashion. We have to work with others and invite them into the fold as allies and advocates for change. In doing so, we change the narrative for community colleges as the nation's best investment in human capital and most powerful equalizer for the disparities that exist. Always focus on the important work of serving students and helping them achieve, irrespective of job titles or the perceived prestige associated with them, and let the importance of the work itself guide us. And I have tried—not always successfully—not to confuse *who I am* with *what I do*, no matter how significant a role I have played. Along the way, we must learn to be resilient, to become patient with ambiguity, and to hold true to our principles and follow our moral convictions. You may discover that the more you help others achieve their goals, the more fulfillment and success you will find in achieving your own.

Diversity and equity do matter. In fact, our democratization depends on it.

References

Campaign for College Opportunity. (2013, December). *The state of Blacks in higher education in California: The persistent opportunity gap.* Los Angeles, CA: Author.

Carnevale, A. P., & Strohl, J. (2013, July). *Separate and unequal: How higher education reinforces the intergenerational reproduction of White racial privilege.* Washington, DC: Georgetown Public Policy Institute, Center on Education and the Workforce.

Cole, S., & Barber, E. G. (2003). *Increasing faculty diversity: The occupational choices of high achieving minority students.* Cambridge, MA: Harvard University Press.

Gutierrez, M., Castañeda, C., & Katsinas, S. G. (2002). Latina/o leadership in community colleges: Issues and challenges. *Community College Journal of Research and Practice, 26,* 297–314.

The Aspen Institute and Achieving the Dream. (2014). *Crisis and opportunity: Aligning the community college presidency with student success.* Washington, DC: Authors.

University of California, Office of the President. (2001, January 3). Personal memo from University of California President Richard Atkinson to University of California Chancellors.

Washington Higher Education Secretariat (WHES). (2013, July). *Diversity in higher education remains an essential national priority.* Published originally in the New York Times, July 1, 2013. Washington, DC: Author.

FRANCISCO C. RODRIGUEZ *is chancellor of Los Angeles Community College District.*

3

This chapter highlights the use of the Equity Scorecard with the Community College of Aurora. The Equity Scorecard is a theory-based strategy that assists community colleges in embedding equity into their institutional norms, practices, and policies.

Developing Agency for Equity-Minded Change

Eric R. Felix, Estela Mara Bensimon, Debbie Hanson, James Gray, Libby Klingsmith

The current urgency in increasing the productivity of higher education provides a political opportunity to make equity for racial and ethnic groups in community colleges a goal that contributes to the national agenda. The Center for Urban Education (CUE)[1] has pioneered the Equity Scorecard, a theory-based strategy consisting of tools, activities, and processes to assist campuses in embedding equity into their structures, policies, and practices. In our work in several states with colleges and systems[2] we have learned that under the right conditions, institutional actors will strive to learn how to change themselves and their own institutions to produce equity in educational outcomes. In this chapter we discuss and demonstrate the development of agency for equity-minded change among institutional actors by focusing on the Community College of Aurora (CCA) as an exemplar. The Community College of Aurora is one of three colleges that took part in "Equity in Excellence: Higher Education for Colorado's Future"[3] a CUE project in partnership with the Western Interstate Commission of Higher Education (WICHE).

Participatory action research (Kemmis & McTaggart, 2005) is the underpinning of the Equity Scorecard's theory of change and this chapter illustrates how its core method, practitioner-led inquiry into everyday routines, supports equity-minded organizational learning and change. Because participatory action research involves practitioners in the study of their own practices, it is an effective way of developing awareness of inequality in outcomes and learning to view inequality as a problem of practice, rather than as a problem of student deficiencies (Bensimon & Malcom, 2012).

New Directions for Community Colleges, no. 172, Winter 2015 © 2015 Wiley Periodicals, Inc.
Published online in Wiley Online Library (wileyonlinelibrary.com) • DOI: 10.1002/cc.20161

25

The implementation of the Equity Scorecard is a joint effort between CUE researchers and a team of faculty, administrators, and staff. CUE's role is to create a structure, including tools and processes that enable insiders to take on the role of researchers and examine student data critically, identify at what points in the academic pathway there is evidence of inequality by race and ethnicity, and design a plan of inquiry to identify practices that have an impact on student outcomes directly (e.g., faculty expertise) or indirectly (e.g., faculty hiring practices).

A few notes about the organization and format of this chapter. The authorship models the collaborative on-the-ground research-practice approach of the Equity Scorecard. The first three authors, Felix, Hanson, and Bensimon, all from CUE, describe the Equity Scorecard process following the conventional academic third person or the collective "we"; James Gray and Libby Klingsmith, both from CCA, speak in the first person to describe how they experienced the Equity Scorecard and what difference it made personally and institutionally. Throughout the chapter, CUE's authors fill in the context that is necessary to give meaning to James's and Libby's comments in relation to the aims and principles of the Equity Scorecard.

Readers will notice that James and Libby's experience of the Equity Scorecard was very positive; as a consequence their commentaries may strike the reader as an "advertisement" for the Equity Scorecard. However, their comments represent "unprompted talk" (Pollock, 2001), culled from conversations, presentations they made to various groups within CCA as well as external audiences, and interviews conducted by CUE as part of our process of documenting the impact of the Equity Scorecard. The Equity Scorecard is a process that is respectful of practitioner knowledge and experience, and we believe it elicits positive responses because the inquiry activities create a sense of purposeful agency. As such, the Equity Scorecard may be welcomed as an antidote to policy reforms that are technocratic or that paint faculty as the obstacle to reform. The action research activities of the Equity Scorecard produce "aha" moments in practitioners that are eye opening as well as empowering when practitioners are able to see that they can change the outcomes of their own practices. These qualities of the scorecard methods increase the likelihood of it being experienced in the positive ways shared by Libby and James.

The Equity Scorecard: A Learning Process of Change

On most college campuses, despite the strong rhetoric on evidence-based decision making, data reports are difficult to decipher and not enough time is dedicated to reading the data, detecting patterns, or asking the next-level questions to dig deeper into the meaning of a number or percentage. The Equity Scorecard bridges the gap between data and action by engaging practitioners in a structured process of action research that involves two kinds of inquiry. First, quantitative analysis of data disaggregated

NEW DIRECTIONS FOR COMMUNITY COLLEGES • DOI: 10.1002/cc

by race and ethnicity is used to identify equity gaps in basic metrics of student progress toward degree attainment. Second, qualitative analysis such as observations, interviews, and document reviews is conducted to investigate practices, structures, and policies through the lens of equity. Teams examine data that are organized into four kinds of educational outcomes: completion (e.g., accumulation of a minimum number of credits per semester), retention (e.g., pass rates in basic skills math courses), excellence (e.g., completing transfer requirements in science, technology, engineering, mathematics fields), and access (e.g., completion of prerequisites for admission into majors leading to high-paying fields). These types of measures are common in national policy- and accountability-oriented initiatives such as Complete College America. However, the important distinction between the Equity Scorecard and big data campaigns is that we put the data in the hands of practitioners and give them the tools to arrive at their own interpretations rather than being told what the data show.

We recognize that on most college campuses it would be nearly impossible to achieve equity without the engagement of practitioners, particularly faculty, in a deep and guided examination of teaching and learning. Too many change initiatives fail because they do not take into account the uniqueness of academic organizations, particularly those reform projects that overlook the primacy of faculty over just about everything that affects educational outcomes.

The Equity Scorecard frames the persistence of inequity in educational outcomes as a problem of institutional performance that calls for the remediation of practices (as well as structures and policies) from the standpoint of equity. This approach requires that institutional actors unlearn normative perspectives that explain academic success as an outcome of students' behaviors, motivations, goal orientation, and sense of self-efficacy (Bensimon, 2007). Instead, practitioners learn to reframe racial/ethnic inequity as a symptom of undetected and unintended institutional dysfunctions and they, individually and collectively, have the power to take action to remediate them.

Within the Equity Scorecard framework, practitioners (e.g., faculty, staff, leaders) are viewed as agents of their own change. The strategy to obtain self-change consists of action research activities designed to help practitioners see what is not working and change their practices to intentionally focus on equity. For example, later James will share what he discovered by pulling apart his hiring practices and how he changed them to be equity focused.

Inequalities in educational outcomes are treated as an indeterminate situation (Dewey, 1938) that calls for investigation. Practitioners actually study such things as how students are advised, analyze policies such as those that govern student eligibility for the honors program, and assess structures such as the transfer center and who is served by it. Inquiry serves as a catalyst for change in practitioners' mental schema. Participants learn to ask: In what ways are my/our practices failing to produce success for such and such students, e.g., Latinos, Blacks, Asian Americans, or American Indians?

The processes through which the activities of the Equity Scorecard are implemented focus on three aspects of learning:

1. Collaborative Learning. Learning is a social act, facilitated by assisted performance, mediated by cultural tools and artifacts, and takes place in communities of practice (Wenger, 1998). Hence, the activities of the Equity Scorecard are carried out by an "evidence team."

2. Double-Loop Learning. Organizational change that is enduring requires double-loop learning, meaning that instead of jumping into problem solving based on the assumption that a problem is understood, institutional actors have to acknowledge that the problem exists and that the reasons for its existence are unknown to them (Argyris & Schön, 1996; Bauman, 2005). Hence, in order to solve the problem of inequity, it must first be labeled as a "problem" that needs to be interrogated in order to craft appropriate solutions. Through a facilitated process, participants learn to resist their natural inclination to assume that they understand the problem in order to open themselves up to learn something new (Bensimon, 2005). Participants are encouraged to pull apart the problem and get to the underlying ideology or theory of the practice that underpins it.

3. Equity-Minded Learning. The eradication of racial inequality in higher education outcomes requires equity-minded practitioners. The characteristics of equity-mindedness are as follows: (a) being race conscious in a critical way, as opposed to color blind; (b) being cognizant of structural and institutional racism as the root cause of inequities as opposed to deficiencies stemming from essentialist perspectives on race or ethnicity; (c) recognizing that to achieve equity it may be necessary to treat individuals unequally as opposed to treating everyone equally; and (d) being able to focus on practices as the source of failure rather than student deficits, e.g., asking what is going on in the transfer center that might discourage African-American students from taking advantage of it, rather than assuming African-American students are not interested in transfer.

In the next section we illustrate how these types of learning are implemented through the Equity Scorecard.

The Equity Scorecard Phases

The Equity Scorecard is organized into five phases: *Laying the Groundwork, Defining the Problem, Assessing Interventions, Implementing Solutions,* and *Evaluating Results.* This chapter shares experiences from the first three phases, which focus heavily on data inquiry, identification of equity gaps, and developing appropriate intervention points. Although the label for the fourth phase, *Implementing Solutions*, may make the Equity Scorecard appear to be a linear process that culminates with the implementation of solutions, in reality change or "solutions" develop continuously, from the very first phase because our learning activities prompt participants to immediately shift attention to their own practices and values. Our conceptualization of change distinguishes the Equity Scorecard from other data-based reform efforts. Accountability-based reform efforts in higher education frame change as a process of implementing technical or structural solutions, e.g., "accelerated remedial education" or "learning communities" to solve problems revealed by data metrics on retention and completion. In the Equity Scorecard, "data" are important not only for what problems they reveal, but also because the social process of making meaning of data is a powerful catalyst to practitioner reflection that leads to self-change. To put it more simply, in data-based initiatives, data are treated discretely from change-oriented solutions. In contrast, we view data-based inquiry as the strategy that makes change happen.

Laying the Groundwork.   The *Laying the Groundwork* phase involves CUE's researchers meeting with campus leaders, typically the president and provost, to explain the process that will take place over 1 or 2 years. One of the most critical activities during this phase is the creation of a team.

Guided by CUE's "Assembling the Evidence Team" tool, campus administrators select team members and leaders who collectively have the characteristics associated with "high learning" (Lorenz, 2012) and cognitively complex teams (Bensimon & Neumann, 1994). The tool helps campus leaders identify individuals who are likely to play one or more of the following roles: analysts, individuals who are good at interpreting data and seeing patterns; interpreters, individuals who will ask "How do we know that . . . .?"; and emotional monitors, individuals who can address the human, personal, and emotional aspects of the team. The "Assembling the Evidence Team" tool delineates ideal team leaders as individuals who are able to create a safe and friendly culture of inquiry, encourage questioning of taken-for-granted knowledge, do not allow individuals to dominate conversations, pose questions to encourage reflection, and are highly organized and task oriented. Institutional researchers are required to be part of the team as the Equity Scorecard relies greatly on numeric data. Institutional researchers who do well with the Equity Scorecard tend not to "get stuck on technical statistical issues, create an environment that allows people to ask seemingly "dumb" questions, and do not assume that everyone can read and interpret data tables in the same way he/she does (Dowd, Malcom, Nakamoto, & Bensimon, 2012).

Finally, "Assembling the Evidence Team" tool provides several prompts to assist leaders appoint individuals who are respected and have a reputation for leadership. Teams with the characteristics described previously are more likely to engage in the following actions: They prioritize data over anecdotal knowledge, are open to the idea that achieving racial equity in educational outcomes is an important and appropriate goal, dig deep into data and know how to interrogate it, and are able to identify points of intervention.

Over time we have learned that the composition of the evidence team influences the extent to which the values, practices, knowledge, and competencies of the Equity Scorecard will become embedded into the campus culture. Our early experiences with the equity scorecard revealed that leaders, without greater guidance, were not as deliberate about the creation of the team, and often we found ourselves with teams of well-meaning individuals who cared deeply about students but lacked the power, influence, and institutional know-how that is necessary to create change from the ground up. We also encountered the all-too-common problem of leaders automatically categorizing the Equity Scorecard as belonging in the "diversity" sphere and thus creating a team of "diversity workers" who do not have the positioning or power needed to make change. The Equity Scorecard focuses on changes in practices, policies, and structures and, sadly, on most campuses, individuals who hold diversity-related positions do not hold academic appointments or are not part of the president's or provost's cabinets; thus they have limited power to make the kinds of changes aimed at by the Equity Scorecard.

The team at Community College of Aurora, which is led by coauthors James Gray, chair of the Mathematics Department, and Libby Klingsmith, coordinator of First Year and Transition Programming, meets the characteristics of an effective team in several ways. The other members of the team include three instructors, the dean of academic affairs, the assistant to the vice president of student affairs, the dean of student success (who early in the process was promoted to vice president of student affairs), the executive director of grants and planning, a career coach, and the director of assessment and institutional research. The team is also diverse in terms of racial, ethnic, and gender composition. Individuals in this team oversee important areas that affect the educational core of the institution as well as all those services that exist to support student success. These individuals have the positional authority and power to convene staff and spread the characteristics of equity-mindedness to campus-wide initiatives of which they are part, such as strategic planning, academic reform, and accreditation self-studies.

Listed next are some examples to illustrate how the CCA team was able to take the Equity Scorecard beyond their 11-member team, an essential element of successful implementation:

- As the chair of the Mathematics Department, James Gray was able to convene the math faculty and engage them in an examination of their syllabi using the Equity Scorecard's "Syllabus Review" protocol. He also adopted the practice of disaggregating data by race and ethnicity to inform the redesign of developmental math courses.
- As coordinator of the First Year and Transition Programming, Libby Klingsmith was able to organize a review of the website and documents

related to advising and to interview advisors to learn how they consider race and ethnicity in their professional practice.

- James and Libby strategically used their institutional status to request time in the regular meetings of the president and her cabinet. They presented updates on the equity scorecard regularly and, through these updates, they introduced specialized language and concepts to institutional leaders. Language and concepts such as equity minded, race conscious, and structural racism are an essential tool of the Equity Scorecard because the attainment of equity requires that practitioners and leaders learn to understand and talk about race as a structural problem. The creation and use of a new language for equity, and what we refer to as "equity-mindedness," is necessary because racial-ethnic inequities often seem natural, overwhelming, or the responsibility of other individuals or institutions (Dowd & Bensimon, 2014).

- They also ensured that the Equity Scorecard work and principles would be incorporated into institutional priorities. As a result, the Equity Scorecard has a strong presence in CCA's new master plan.

Defining the Problem.   In the *Defining the Problem* phase, the evidence team participates in a 2-day event organized by CUE's researchers and project specialists to introduce the evidence team to the scorecard's specialized language (e.g., equity-mindedness), its principles and theory of change, and the meaning of equity and what makes it different from diversity and equality.

The team members participate in a variety of exercises to learn how to interrogate numeric data and, most important, how to interpret data from an equity perspective. Using CUE's Benchmarking Equity and Student Success Tool (BESST), the CCA team reviewed data on completion, year-to-year retention, enrollment and success in gatekeeper courses, and timely credit accumulation. Among the things they learned was that full-time African-American students, compared to other groups, had a lower rate of degree or transfer attainment within 3 years of enrolling.

To illustrate the role disaggregated data play in shining the light on equity gaps, we draw on reflections from coauthor James Gray, who is the chair of the math department as well as the co–team leader of CCA's Equity Scorecard team.

> James: When I looked at the retention and completion data by race and ethnicity, it was a "big surprise." As chair of the Mathematics Department, I had always felt a sense of pride in our success. The year before we started the Equity Scorecard, we became part of the National Community College Benchmark Project,[4] which is still ongoing and includes 200 community colleges. Our department placed in the 90th percentile of community colleges in college algebra success rates. But when I looked at the disaggregated data it was a punch in the gut when we got the results back and saw that African-American

students in developmental courses were not passing; were overrepresented in remedial courses, underrepresented in college algebra, and their overall success rate in developmental math was under 50%.

Even though James is the chair of the math department he had not had an opportunity to look at data disaggregated by race and ethnicity and when he did, he realized that there were serious problems. Not having access to student performance data disaggregated by race and ethnicity is not unusual because disaggregation by race and ethnicity is not a standard operating procedure on most colleges campuses. Often colleges aggregate all students of Color into a single category such as "non-White," which is just as problematic as not disaggregating because it hides interracial differences in outcomes. For example, if CCA had aggregated all students of Color into underrepresented minorities, they would have not realized that African-American students were experiencing the greatest inequities in basic indicators of academic progress.

Prior to the Equity Scorecard, the disaggregation of data had not been done routinely at CCA. Consequently, discussions about the "color" of student success were not common. Libby Klingsmith, coauthor and co-team leader, shares how the availability of disaggregated data encouraged new and necessary conversations based on evidence.

> Libby: I came here 3 years ago; nothing like this had happened on campus. To be able to discuss student success in terms of race and ethnicity, moving from an emotionally charged conversation to a discussion based on disaggregated institutional data.

Another obstacle to meaningful use of data is the ways in which it is organized and communicated. Institutional research offices spend a great deal of time preparing compliance reports such as for the Integrated Postsecondary Education Data System (IPEDS), leaving them with little time to create reports that are user friendly and conducive to critical discussions. Another problem is the lack of time and assistance to make sense of data. For example, Libby observed: "We don't often take the time to have very deep and meaningful conversations about data. When we do look at data, it tends to be very quick because we are trying to make decisions."

Numeric data are used in the Equity Scorecard to uncover fine-grained racialized patterns of inequality that help participants make decisions on where to intervene strategically. However, on most college campuses we have found that participants, from presidents to counselors, tend to skip problem defining and jump directly into solutions. Again we turn to Libby,

> Libby: There is a tendency for people to quickly go into solutions and not stay in the inquiry phase. As a team leader, keeping colleagues rooted in the data rather than jumping to a solution was a challenge.

NEW DIRECTIONS FOR COMMUNITY COLLEGES • DOI: 10.1002/cc

Figure 3.1.   African-American Equity Gaps and Goals from CCA's
Equity Scorecard Report. The lefthand square shows the 3-year
graduation/transfer rate for full-time African-American students who
entered CCA in 2009. The righthand square shows how many
additional African Americans would graduate/transfer if their success
rate went up from 29.7% to 40.4%, which was the graduation/transfer
rate for the highest performing group.

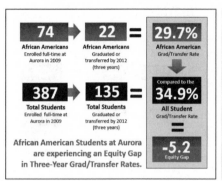 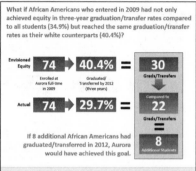

Source: "Community College of Aurora Equity Scorecard Report for Retention and Completion,"
by the Community College of Aurora Equity Scorecard Evidence Team and Estela Bensimon, 2013.
Used with permission of the authors.

The *Defining the Problem* phase culminates with the selection of a focal effort. In CUE's language "focal effort" refers to identifying a specific
student population, their equity gap, and the performance level they must
reach to achieve equity. The specificity of the focal effort avoids the tendency toward abstract goal statements such as "improve the success of all
underrepresented students" that are too often found in strategic plans. Se-
lecting a focal effort requires that the evidence team name the additional
number of students from their selected group that would need to succeed
in order to achieve equity (as shown in Figures 3.1 and 3.2). The focal effort is written out in detail for two reasons: first, so that the team members
are able to speak about it knowledgeably and second, so that anyone who
reads the report is not left confused or guessing about the goals moving
forward. Although the written version, provided in Table 3.1, may strike
some as simplistic, we have learned that translating a data table to a written statement is often a challenge for participants who are not accustomed
to articulating the story that is represented by numeric data. Furthermore,
it is difficult to make the transition from seeing the data as numbers and
figures on paper to understanding that they represent actual students that
faculty and staff interact with daily. By naming the number of focal effort
students needed to achieve equity, the team is creating a new "story" about
the future they would like to construct. The two figures are excerpted from
CCA's Equity Scorecard report along with their written explanation.

NEW DIRECTIONS FOR COMMUNITY COLLEGES • DOI: 10.1002/cc

Figure 3.2.   Hispanic/Latino Equity Gaps and Goals from CCA's Equity
Scorecard Report. The lefthand square shows the 3-year
graduation/transfer rate for full-time Hispanic/Latino students who
entered CCA in 2009. The righthand square shows how many
additional Hispanic/Latinos would graduate/transfer if their success rate
went up from 22.2% to 40.4%, which was the graduation/transfer rate
for the highest performing group.

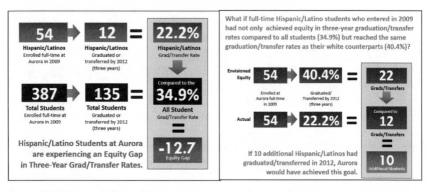

Source: "Community College of Aurora Equity Scorecard Report for Retention and Completion,"
by the Community College of Aurora Equity Scorecard Evidence Team and Estela Bensimon, 2013.
Used with permission of the authors.

Table 3.1   Text Descriptions of African-American and Hispanic/Latino
Equity Gaps and Goals from CCA's Equity Scorecard Report.

Equity Gap: Of the 74 full-time **African Americans** who enrolled at Aurora in 2009, only 22, or 29.7%, earned a degree, certificate, or transferred by 2012. In comparison, the all student average graduation/transfer rate for the same cohort was 34.9%; and for Whites, the highest achieving group on this metric, it was 40.4%. The difference reveals a **–5.2 and –10.7 percentage point gap respectively.**	**Equity Gap:** Of the 54 full-time **Hispanic/Latinos** who enrolled at Aurora in 2009, 12, or 22.2%, earned a degree, certificate, or transferred by 2012. In comparison, the all student average graduation/transfer rate for the same cohort was 34.9%; and for Whites, the highest achieving group on this metric, it was 40.4%. The difference reveals a **–12.7 and –18.2 percentage point gap respectively.**
Equity Goal: By 2017, African Americans' 3-year graduation rate will be 40.4%, which is equal to the graduation/transfer rate for Whites.	**Equity Goal:** By 2017, Hispanic/Latinos' 3-year graduation rate will be 40.4%, which is equal to the graduation/transfer rate for Whites.

Source: "Community College of Aurora Equity Scorecard Report for Retention and Completion,"
by the Community College of Aurora Equity Scorecard Evidence Team and Estela Bensimon, 2013.
Used with permission of the authors.

CCA selected two focal efforts to improve 3-year graduation/transfer rates for African-American and Hispanic/Latino full-time students using 2009 as their baseline year. The focal efforts were selected through a collaborative decision-making process based on campus context at the time of the scorecard process, as well as considering the institution's strategic plan and state's completion initiative. In the figures, the left-hand squares show the 3-year graduation/transfer rate for full-time students who are African American (Figure 3.1) and Hispanic/Latino (Figure 3.2). The right-hand squares show how many more African Americans (Figure 3.1) and Hispanic/Latinos (Figure 3.2) would graduate/transfer if their success rate went up from 29.7% and 22.2% respectively to 40.4%, which was the graduation/transfer rate of the highest achieving group.

CCA's team decided to set the equity goal for African Americans and Hispanic/Latinos to 40.4%, the rate for Whites, rather than to 34.9%, the average rate for all students, because by setting a higher goal all students would benefit. Although the Equity Scorecard focuses on racial/ethnic equity, the goal-setting process as demonstrated for this metric benefits all students because it builds an expectation that all full-time students will achieve at least a 40.4% completion rate within 3 years. The team acknowledged that a 40.4% completion rate is still below optimal performance; however, in the pragmatic spirit of the Equity Scorecard it was important to set a goal that the team felt was attainable and more likely to motivate action than a goal that is perceived as wishful thinking.

When viewing gaps such as the ones depicted in the figures and table, it is a challenge to keep team members from getting into a "problem-solving" mode. Double-loop learning (Argyris & Schön, 1996), one of the aims of the Equity Scorecard, requires that practitioners focus on understanding how practices that are taken for granted are often racialized in their impact. However, double-loop learning is difficult and requires tools and coaching. To facilitate double-loop learning evidence team members move into the third phase of the Equity Scorecard, labeled *Assessing Interventions* and learn, both for themselves and on behalf of their institutions, by becoming researchers of their own and the campus practices. The next section describes the implementation of this phase.

Assessing Interventions. The term "interventions" is used to refer to institutionalized structures, systems, practices, and policies such as tutoring centers, early alert systems, first-year experience, learning communities, and mandatory assessment in basic skills. Even though such structures are not typically viewed as "interventions," we label them so to underscore that their purpose is to mediate student success. The problem is that they do not always "intervene" in culturally responsive ways to support student success and, if left unexamined, often, even though without intention, reproduce inequality. Therefore it is important to ask: How does such and such program, office, or policy work? Who benefits? Who is disadvantaged?

Thus when assessing interventions the evidence team identifies institutional resources that exist on campus that have the potential of ameliorating the equity gaps represented in the focal effort(s) identified in the *Defining the Problem* phase, but rather than assuming these resources work equally well for all students the team members develop an inquiry plan to pull them apart and learn in what ways they work for African-American, Latino, or Hmong students, for example. The purpose of inquiry is for practitioners to "walk" through the structures, programs, and various offices and try to experience them from the standpoint of first-generation students from marginalized communities. The CCA team first had to consider what "interventions" might have the greatest impact on improving 3-year graduation outcomes for full-time African-Americans and Latino/a students.

Wanting to further unpack the inequities in mathematics found in the previous phase, the team was compelled to focus on Math-121-College Algebra. The course was known to be a barrier to transfer and graduation. The decision to focus intervention efforts in mathematics addressed both the disparities in educational outcomes locally while incorporating the state's large goal of improved completion. The inquiry activities that were carried out to assess how "mathematics" at CCA works in general and how they might be experienced by African-American and Latino students more specifically are described next.

Developmental Math Courses.   Using CUE's Syllabus Review Protocol, the evidence team assessed course syllabi, asking: What do the documents intentionally or unintentionally communicate to students? What is the tone of the document? Is the information communicated clearly? Does it make assumptions about what students should know? The evidence team learned how a syllabus can affect, either positively or negatively, students' beliefs about their capacity to succeed. Although all syllabi had positive aspects, each also had room for improvement. The team members noticed that syllabi tended to have hidden assumptions, unclear expectations, technical language, and a disengaged tone.

An example of a finding is the statement, "As a college student you need to accept the responsibility for your own learning." Although this statement was written with the positive intention of motivating students to be proactive in their learning, it could be interpreted as though the instructor is not responsible for engaging or providing them with the tools to learn. The team member who reviewed this syllabus commented, "This statement made me feel like I did something wrong before the class starts." Moreover, the wording of the statement makes the assumption that the student has an equivalent understanding of what it means to be a college student, which disproportionately affects first-generation students and hence students of Color. In addition to finding that the language in syllabi was often not student friendly, there was "little to no mention of diversity, inclusiveness, or empowerment" in the syllabi.

NEW DIRECTIONS FOR COMMUNITY COLLEGES • DOI: 10.1002/cc

The inquiry activities brought into greater awareness ways in which the disciplinary culture of math might reinforce students' feelings of inadequacy as mathematicians. Admonishing students by telling them "you should know this" seemed a common practice. The language of syllabi at times felt as if the instructor was "screaming" at students even though that was not the instructor's intent. Being cognizant that the tone of the syllabus may be different from the tone in which a faculty member discusses it, the team followed up the syllabi review with observations of how math instructors talked about the syllabus during the first day of class.

Using CUE's Observation Protocol, members of the evidence team visited a few math classrooms on the first day of the semester to learn how faculty members communicated with students, how welcoming the classroom was to students, what was discussed on the first session, and how academic norms were established through the introduction of the syllabus. The team members saw how much impact the first day of class can have on students' beliefs that they are capable of being successful. The instructors whose syllabi were negatively reviewed tended to deliver information about the course in general terms or to gloss over information students would need to "accept responsibility for their own learning" as many instructors seemed to expect.

The observations produced an unexpected "aha" moment about the racial disadvantages imposed by the math instructional approach used by CCA instructors. CCA's math faculty members use a procedural teaching approach in developmental courses. It just so happens that the procedural approach is also used by the math instructors at CCA's predominantly White feeder high school; however, at the predominantly minority high school math teachers use the conceptual/discovery approach. This finding helped team members see how "race" is implicated in the curriculum and pedagogy and how it may be contributing to lower rates of success for African Americans and Latinos who are unfamiliar with the procedural approach.

The Value of Guided Inquiry

In reflecting about the use of formal protocols to examine practices, Libby said, "These protocols make things that you had never seen before so obvious. You find yourself looking around and asking, why was I unaware of this?" The inquiry activities enabled a new perspective on student success. As James shared, "[Inquiry] gets you to come from a completely different point of view, and it gets you thinking about your students in a complete different way. Protocols for observing, studying the syllabus, analyzing the website help participants see in very concrete ways the changes that are within their power to make."

At its most successful, guided inquiry helps practitioners change themselves. Inquiry enables practitioners to see, for example, their syllabus from the perspective of a student and when they realize that the syllabus communicates more effectively all the ways in which the student can fail rather than succeed, it is far more likely that the practitioner will change it than if they went to a workshop where they heard someone lecture about the elements of a good syllabus.

In the case of James the inquiry process made him realize how implicit bias shaped his hiring practices.

> James: The process led me to face the fact that over a 10-year period I had never hired an African-American adjunct to teach College Algebra, something I found very difficult to be confronted with. It became clear during a review of the hiring practices of full-time and part-time faculty that the strategies used to recruit faculty disadvantaged candidates of Color. As an example, a recruiting strategy for both full-time and part-time faculty has been to contact department chairs from CCA's sister community colleges for referrals. Although this strategy met the needs of finding faculty to fill positions, the strategy all but ensured the pool would not be diverse.

James's realization led to concrete changes in recruitment as well as in the interview process. For example, he conducted many more screening interviews. Candidates who were invited to campus had to demonstrate how they would explain the syllabus on the first day of class. The syllabus inquiry activity had helped him and his colleagues see the importance of the syllabus as a cultural practice that influences how students feel about the class, the faculty member, and their likelihood of success. These changes helped them identify candidates who were able to show they cared for students and took their success as a personal responsibility. African-American and Latino faculty have been added to the math department since the implementation of the scorecard.

Becoming Equity Minded

Developing the schema of equity-mindedness is the ultimate objective of the Equity Scorecard; however, this is one of the most challenging aspects of CUE's work because it requires that practitioners, the majority of whom are White, engage the "race question" and the privileges and power derived from their own racial identity (Dowd & Bensimon, 2014). On most campuses "color blindness" is the status quo and most find it more comfortable to talk about diversity as an institutional asset or to focus on low income, rather than race, as a source of inequity. Equity-mindedness requires that practitioners accept that higher education as an institution is racialized and that structural racism is produced by everyday practices that are grounded, as James indicates, on norms and rules that privilege Whites.

In the excerpts that follow James and Libby discuss their own evolving equity-mindedness. In the first excerpt James relates what he learned by observing a class taught by an African-American faculty member who was also in the Equity Scorecard evidence team.

> James: In doing the Equity Scorecard I realized that there is an expectation that everyone function according to the norms and rules of White dominant culture. In my view, this manifests itself most strongly in communication style. The dominant culture highly values the individual, and as such avoids directives that may appear to take away individual liberty. For example, I now see that it is common for a White teacher to talk about homework using language such as, "if you want to do well in the course, you must do your homework." In other words, homework is a choice with consequences. An instructor of Color is much more likely to use language such as, "I expect you to do your homework," and to follow up with the student who does not complete it. Therefore, when I work with faculty now, we talk about strategies specific to race and ethnicity. It is important for faculty to get out of their comfort zone and set a direct expectation, and then to follow that up with appropriate support.

At first glance, James's realization of differences in communication styles and his conclusion that faculty of Color are more direct about their expectations than Whites may sound essentialist. Needless to say, directive language is not a natural attribute of people of Color. However, faculty of Color may have greater awareness that caring is communicated by creating a structure that communicates clear expectations and substantive support. James's noticing of directive vs. nondirective language calls attention to the importance of awareness of meaning in what faculty say and how they say it. Context and identity are also important elements of meaning making. The directive language noticed by James is mediated by the racial identity of the instructor and the cultural practices of that particular classroom. James's new awareness of the silent expectation that everyone function according to the "norms and rules of White dominant culture" signifies the development of equity-mindedness and his evolving identity as he likes to put it, "a first-generation equity worker."

Another aspect of demonstrating equity-mindedness is by considering how one's position and power can be used intentionally "to ingrain more institutional members with a sense of *agency* for equity" (Bishop, 2014, p. 208). A semester into the process, Libby and James decided to hold an All College Forum with over 80 campus members. During the event they presented on conceptual aspects of the scorecard process, specifically discussing equity-mindedness. As facilitators, they were intentional in designing an event to be dialogue based. Not everyone was comfortable at the start of the event. For example, rather than talking about racial inequities, someone wanted to spend time talking about reverse racism. A few people brought up color blindness as a better way to work with students.

James: Looking back on our meetings, I'm really proud of what our college was able to accomplish and my own professional growth. Knowing that you must be a leader on a highly charged discussion of racial bias creates a lot of anxiety, but I've learned that doing it well is just like anything else; it takes practice. To get that practice meant the leadership of our college allowing us to be put in challenging circumstances where we were likely to offend people. My wish for others in this process is that they may experience the same expectation being such a leader.

Earlier we mentioned that a challenge to equity-mindedness is the lack of structures and competency to engage in "race talk." James's observation that "it takes practice" to be equity minded makes sense and the Equity Scorecard is an effort to create a process that routinizes race talk through the engagement of practitioners in the study of how they and their institutions go about the everyday performance of higher education.

So What? Does the Equity Scorecard Make a Difference?

Although the Equity Scorecard has been very successful at CCA, there have been instances of pushback from faculty and others who question the focus on racial equity. Precisely because "race talk" was rare at CCA, early in the scorecard process Libby and James noticed a hesitancy—sometimes outright resistance—to treat race as a central issue of teaching and learning. There was also a resistance from campus practitioners to disaggregate data based on race and ethnicity when examining student success metrics. Although the ambivalence about race talk has not been fully resolved, there are signs of important changes, including: all data are now routinely disaggregated, equity goals by race and ethnicity are transparent, diversity in hiring is a stated priority, and three of the five new math faculty hired are people of Color.

We are often asked, what evidence do you have that changes such as those made by CCA will close the equity gaps experienced by Latinos, Blacks, American Indians, and Asian Pacific Islanders? And of course we are not able to claim having "moved the needle" in small or big ways. However, we can point out that Equity Scorecard campuses like CCA are engaging in two essential equity practices that are not common on most campuses: they set clear and measurable goals by race and ethnicity and they disaggregate their data routinely (Witham, Malcom-Piqueux, Dowd, & Bensimon, 2015). Institutional actors pay attention to what is measured and reported publicly; thus, at a minimum these two measures create the conditions for equity as an indicator of accountability and overall institutional performance.

Finally, the CCA engagement with the Equity Scorecard demonstrates that when practitioners are empowered with language to talk critically about race and given the tools to shift to equity-minded action, they can bring about the kinds of changes that cumulatively transform the teaching and learning environment in ways that are more responsive to the success of historically marginalized students.

Notes

1. For additional information on our research and publications, see http://cue.usc.edu.
2. The Equity Scorecard has been implemented in the University of Wisconsin System, the Pennsylvania State System of Higher Education, and individual campuses in California, Colorado, Nevada, Indiana, and New York.
3. Equity in Excellence was made possible by grants from the Ford Foundation and the Bill and Melinda Gates Foundation.
4. For more information on the project, visit https://www.nccbp.org/.

References

Argyris, C., & Schön, D. A. (1996). *Organizational learning II: Theory, method, and practice*. Reading, PA: Addison-Wesley.

Bauman, G. L. (2005). Promoting organizational learning in higher education to achieve equity in educational outcomes. In A. Kezar (Ed.), *New Directions for Higher Education: No. 131. Organizational learning in education* (pp. 23–35). San Francisco, CA: Jossey-Bass.

Bensimon, E. M. (2005). Closing the achievement gap in higher education: An organizational learning perspective. In A. J. Kezar (Ed.), *New Directions for Higher Education: No. 131. Organizational learning in education* (pp. 99–111). San Francisco, CA: Jossey-Bass.

Bensimon, E. M. (2007). The underestimated significance of practitioner knowledge in the scholarship of student success. *Review of Higher Education, 30*(4), 441–469.

Bensimon, E. M., & Malcom, L. E. (2012). *Confronting equity issues on campus*. Sterling, VA: Stylus.

Bensimon, E. M., & Neumann, A. (1994). *Redesigning collegiate leadership: Teams and teamwork in higher education*. Baltimore, MD: Johns Hopkins University Press.

Bishop, R. (2014). *Language and identity in critical sensegiving: Journeys of higher education equity agents* (Unpublished doctoral dissertation). University of Southern California, Los Angeles.

Dewey, J. (1938). *Logic: The theory of inquiry*. New York: Henry Holt.

Dowd, A. C., & Bensimon, E. M. (2014). *Engaging the race question: Accountability and equity in U.S. higher education*. New York, NY: Teachers College Press.

Dowd, A. C., Malcom, L., Nakamoto, J., & Bensimon, E. M. (2012). Institutional researchers as teachers and equity advocates. In E. M. Bensimon & L. Malcom (Eds.), *Confronting equity issues on campus: Implementing the equity scorecard in theory and practice* (pp. 191–215). Sterling, VA: Stylus.

Kemmis, S., & McTaggart, R. (2005). Participatory action research: Communicative action and the public sphere. In N. K. Denzin & Y. S. Lincoln (Eds.), *Handbook of qualitative research* (pp. 559–603). Thousand Oaks, CA, Sage Publications.

Lorenz, G. L. (2012). Scorecard teams as high learning groups: Group learning and the value of group learning. In E. M. Bensimon & L. Malcom (Eds.), *Confronting equity issues on campus: Implementing the equity scorecard in theory and practice* (pp. 45–63). Sterling, VA: Stylus.

Pollock, M. (2001). How the question we ask most about race in education is the very question we most suppress. *Educational Researcher, 30*(9), 2–12.

Wenger, E. (1998). *Communities of practice: Learning, meaning, and identity.* New York, NY: Cambridge University Press.

Witham, K., Malcom-Piqueux, L. E., Dowd, A. C., & Bensimon, E. M. (2015). *America's unmet promise: The imperative for equity in higher education.* Washington, DC: Association of American Colleges and Universities.

ERIC R. FELIX *is a doctoral student in the Urban Education Policy program at the University of Southern California's Rossier School of Education*

ESTELA MARA BENSIMON *is a professor of higher education and codirector of the Center for Urban Education (CUE) at the USC Rossier School of Education.*

DEBBIE HANSON *is a project administrator in the Center for Urban Education at the USC Rossier School of Education.*

JAMES GRAY *is the chair of the Mathematics Department at the Community College of Aurora.*

LIBBY KLINGSMITH *is the associate dean of Early College High Schools at Aims Community College.*

4

At a time when the nation is focusing so much attention on college completion, what do we know about how students are completing their community college programs? Does the open-access mission of community colleges translate into equitable outcomes? Pathways to Results (PTR) engages practitioners in using data to close equity gaps for student groups historically underserved by postsecondary education. This chapter describes the experiences of practitioners at Richland Community College who implemented PTR to improve student access, outcomes, and equity in an associate degree nursing program.

Pathways to Results: How Practitioners Address Student Access, Outcomes, and Equity in an Associate Degree Nursing Program

Jessica Pickel, Debra D. Bragg

What Is Pathways to Results?

In 2009 the Office of Community College Research and Leadership (OC-CRL), University of Illinois at Urbana-Champaign, developed Pathways to Results (PTR) to help practitioners to improve career pathways that begin in K–12, adult education, or workforce training and extend to college and ultimately employment. Learning from researchers from the Center for Urban Education (CUE) about their Equity Scorecard (Felix et al., Chapter 3), OCCRL created PTR to help practitioners understand how diverse student groups are experiencing their collegiate programs of study and use data to bring about improvements that yield more equitable outcomes than in the past. PTR's approach to inquiry integrates participatory action research, developmental evaluation (Patton, 2011), and continuous

The Office of Community College Research and Leadership (OCCRL) would like to thank the Illinois Community College Board, Springfield, Illinois, for its generous and sustained funding since July 1, 2009 to make the development, implementation, and scale-up of Pathways to Results possible.

New Directions for Community Colleges, no. 172, Winter 2015 © 2015 Wiley Periodicals, Inc.
Published online in Wiley Online Library (wileyonlinelibrary.com) • DOI: 10.1002/cc.20162

43

improvement methods to help practitioners to gather, analyze, and use data to identify and resolve equity gaps.

Why Focus on Pathways and Results?

With college completion rates falling relative to other nations (see Kanter, Ochoa, Nassif, & Chong, 2011), improving access and completion of college is a critical policy focus of the Obama Administration. Although this emphasis on college completion is logical and important, it is problematic if access is not given an equally high priority. Left unchecked, an emphasis on college completion without attention to access may lead to greater inequities among student groups than that have existed in the past. Postsecondary educators throughout the country need methods to understand how their programs and practices, already stratified by race, ethnicity, and income, affect student outcomes. Because community colleges are a primary gateway to college for underserved students, it is especially important that outcomes attainment is fair and equitable in this setting.

Improving pathways to and through college is a compelling idea to policy makers and practitioners throughout the world (Bathmaker, 2014; Bragg, 2014; Wheelahan, 2014). The notion of "career pathways" that emphasize skills and knowledge that enable students to fulfill their short- and long-term career goals is growing in popularity in the United States (see Bragg, Dresser, & Smith, 2012). By providing skills needed to obtain employment and advance in a career, while providing opportunities for students to return to college to obtain additional postsecondary credentials, career pathways offer the potential for increased social and economic mobility for diverse learners. The notion of a never-ending, iterative education-to-employment-to-education-to-employment cycle fits with the complex lives that people live, moving back and forth from education to employment, but this is not the way educational systems are built. Implementation of career pathways calls for more flexible yet customized approaches to curriculum and instruction than postsecondary education has offered historically. Counter to the notion of tracking that sorts students into standardized curricula that often limit opportunities (depending on the track to which students are assigned), career pathways customize educational options and support students to fulfill their evolving education and career aspirations. They enable students to enter and exit programs of study to acquire college credits and credentials as they progress through education to employment. Philosophically and operationally, career pathways recognize that individuals desire and require opportunities to learn throughout their working lives, albeit throughout their entire lifetimes.

How Does Pathways to Results (PTR) Work?

The PTR methodology emphasizes five critical processes, beginning with (a) the engagement and commitment of practitioners and partners, and

Figure 4.1.   The Pathways to Results Methodology

continuing with (b) equity and outcomes assessment, (c) process assessment, (d) process improvement, and (e) review and reflection (see Figure 4.1).

Believing that student success is facilitated through a broad-based, stakeholder approach, PTR begins with *engagement and commitment* through the formation of a coalition of practitioners, including community college and other educators (e.g., Kindergarten through grade 12, adult, university), as well as students, employers, community leaders, and other stakeholders who map the career pathway programs that are the focus of the PTR process.

Equity and outcomes assessment examines disaggregated student data to identify problems with or barriers to career pathway programs that have the potential to better serve student groups. This phase of the process requires open-mindedness and is characterized by the introduction and encouragement of practitioners to be equity minded (again, see Felix et al., Chapter 3 in this volume). In conducting equity and outcomes assessment, practitioners recognize "'deficit thinking' that sometimes characterizes discussions of outcomes... [At this stage, PTR] teams can move from the idea that 'if we had better students, we would have better outcomes, to the idea that 'if we create better processes, our students will demonstrate better outcomes'" (Harmon, Liss, & Umbricht, 2012, p. 3).

Process assessment allows PTR teams to investigate and document on a deep and nuanced level how processes integral to career pathway programs currently work in order to determine how and why they fall short in serving all student groups. Mapping how processes work helps point to gaps and inadequacies in processes that disadvantage groups of students. Luckily, the tools that enable practitioners to map existing processes can be used to map new ones, so this phase of PTR includes mapping new processes.

Process improvement and evaluation set into motion a plan to implement, evaluate, and improve career pathways on a continuous basis. This stage of the process is typically familiar to practitioners because they are comfortable with planning and excited to make improvements. What is different with PTR is that the decisions that practitioners make are grounded in data that substantiate practitioners' plans to reduce inequities between groups and raise performance for all learners.

Review and reflection uses storytelling as a means of engaging practitioners in reflecting on what they are doing to improve programs and create more equitable outcomes. Representing a form of double-loop learning (Argyris, 1993), stories engender discussion among practitioners holding diverse perspectives, including biases and stereotypes, that need to surface to "imagine new perspectives and new worlds" (Denning, 2011, p. xvii).

Implementation of PTR in Illinois

In the sixth year of PTR implementation, 46 of 48 Illinois community colleges have received a small grant from the Illinois Community College Board to implement one or more PTR projects. An excellent example of how one team has used PTR to improve a career pathway program is Richland Community College in Decatur, Illinois. A description of how Richland implemented PTR and what practitioners have learned through their engagement with the process follows, beginning with the Richland PTR team's implementation of the engagement and commitment process.

Engagement and Commitment. The dean of workforce development administers and coordinates all Perkins Program Grant activities with other areas of Richland Community College. She introduced PTR as an opportunity for the associate degree nursing (ADN) program to engage internal and external stakeholders in a grant-funded continuous improvement process that emphasizes evidence-based decision making, partnerships, and equity. As one of the college's largest accredited career and technical education (CTE) programs, the ADN program is experienced and knowledgeable about how to collect and use data to provide evidence of student learning, identify areas of improvement, and inform decision making. Despite these strengths, it was not common practice for the ADN program to disaggregate data to determine if equity gaps exist among diverse learner groups.

Prior to submitting an application for a PTR grant, a group of college administrators met to develop an initial problem statement. The group determined that poor communication of admission requirements limited access for students from multiple entry points (e.g., high school, adult education, the workforce). If students from these entry points had the information needed to enroll and work toward admission, the program would be more reflective of the college's student population.

To attain a greater understanding of the perceived problem, stakeholders representing local employers; adult, secondary, and postsecondary

NEW DIRECTIONS FOR COMMUNITY COLLEGES • DOI: 10.1002/cc

education; and the local workforce investment board (LWIB) were invited to engage in conversations about the ADN program's strengths, weaknesses, and opportunities related to student outcomes and equity. The group determined that the program had an opportunity to improve access and transition at multiple entry points by increasing community outreach and education to inform prospective students about career options, the nursing profession, Richland's ADN program, and available support services.

Data would later reveal that the program also needed to address issues of completion. External partners provided insight into how to serve their constituents, but to address issues of completion, nursing faculty were later engaged in discussions about equity and process improvement.

Data Collection and Process Mapping. To identify where equity gaps may exist, the group explored the relationships between student characteristics and student outcomes by collecting and disaggregating program and institutional data related to program admission, semester-to-semester retention, and associate's degree completion. Enrollment data from secondary education and adult education nursing programs were also collected and reviewed. Given that the Richland Community College student population is approximately 83% White, 15% African American, 1% Asian, and 1% Hispanic, the ADN program investigated the following questions:

- Does the nursing applicant pool reflect the racial-ethnic demographics of the college?
- Does the admitted nursing cohort reflect the racial-ethnic demographics of the college?
- How do the numbers of recent high school graduates and male students applying to and transitioning into the ADN program compare to their representation within the college?
- Is retention and completion equitable among these various student subgroups?

Using tools from OCCRL's PTR website, the team disaggregated student data by a number of characteristics, including race/ethnicity, socioeconomic status, gender, age, and special populations as defined by the Perkins IV law. Despite the work of several individuals, including the college's database systems staff, there were several areas for which the college had limited data. Due to the college's change in processes and application forms, information about college students with disabilities, limited English proficiency, and parental status were not available. Discussions during statewide meetings revealed that many colleges encountered similar challenges. Internal discussions have continued about this concern, but the college has yet to identify a mechanism to collect the Perkins IV special population data without infringing on students' privacy.

The initial data collected and analyzed revealed the following:

New Directions for Community Colleges • DOI: 10.1002/cc

- Between spring 2010 and spring 2012, African-American students comprised approximately 10% of students applying and admitted, compared to 15% of the college student population. Thus, White students were overrepresented in the applicant pools and admitted cohorts.
- Between spring 2010 and spring 2012, recent high school graduates between the ages of 18 and 25 made up only 30.5% of the applicant pool compared to 57.9% of the college student population.
- Male students represented only 10% of the students applying between spring 2010 and spring 2012 but they made up nearly 39% of the college student population.
- Between spring 2010 and fall 2011, the first-to-second semester retention rate of White students was considerably higher than that of African-American students and 18–19 year olds. Of the male students admitted during the same period, 100% enrolled in the second semester, compared to 75% of females.
- Between fall 2007 and spring 2010, the average completion rate was 65.4%, falling below the program's internal 70% completion target.
- White students exceeded the average completion rate, whereas the completion rates of two groups, African-American students and recent high school graduates, were considerably lower than the average.

These findings led to questions about how students learn about the ADN program, who they rely upon for information, and what other information is needed in the college search and admission process. To answer these questions, the PTR team developed and administered surveys to three groups: high school students applying to the dual credit nurse assistant training program, Fall 2012 ADN applicants, and district high school guidance counselors.

Prospective dual credit nurse assistant training students from rural, urban, and suburban district high schools were surveyed during a campus visit, using an electronic survey developed by PTR team members. Students were asked about their interest in nursing, knowledge of the training and education required, plans after graduation, and resources used and needed to assist them in the college search process. Students were provided a list of commonly used resources and asked to rank how often they were referenced in the college search process and how important other sources might be to their search. Students could list additional information sources that might be important. Students were also given the option to disclose their racial-ethnic background and their parent(s)'/guardian(s)' highest level of schooling. Thirty-eight percent of the surveyed high school students self-identified as African American and over half could be classified as first generation. Students relied heavily on high school guidance counselors, parents, and college admission representatives for college information. Fifty-five percent of surveyed students thought a bachelor's degree or higher was needed to become a registered nurse. To learn more about the

ADN program, students stated they would like to have access to campus visits, faculty members, and current students.

Prior to their spring counselor academy, high school guidance counselors were asked to complete an electronic survey developed by the college PTR team members. Guidance counselors were asked about their knowledge of Richland's nursing program, common reasons students give for pursuing nursing at other institutions, resources used to get more information about Richland's program, and how important other sources might be for students, parents, and counselors. The survey revealed that high school guidance counselors relied heavily on the general Richland advisors and the program website for information, but 62% agreed that conversations with a nursing faculty member were "very important." After the survey, several PTR team members led the counselors in a discussion about the processes used to advise high school students interested in nursing. The processes used and resources accessed varied by counselor, but the discussion revealed that counselors felt students need more exposure to the job opportunities available within health care and information about the education required.

The 43 students applying for admission to the Fall 2012 semester were also invited to complete an electronic survey developed by PTR team members. Twenty-two students responded to questions about their educational background and intentions, current employment status and work intentions if admitted, employer support of plans to pursue nursing, resources used to obtain information about the program, and resources important for other prospective nursing students. The majority of respondents worked up to 30 hours per week while completing prerequisite coursework, and if admitted, they intended to continue that workload. The data also showed that ADN applicants relied heavily on college advisors and peers for program information. They cited information sessions delivered in an online learning platform and conversations with faculty members and current ADN students as other useful information sources.

The issue of retention and completion required the input of nursing faculty. Two PTR team members met with the nursing faculty to review completion data, discuss possible contributing factors, and map their academic intervention process. The program's first semester experienced the highest attrition, leading many faculty to ask why students were leaving. The nursing program director shared that whereas some withdrawals occur for academic difficulties, more than 50% of students withdrew for personal reasons or to change their college major. Faculty stated that students need more information pertaining to the program's rigor so that they can adequately prepare themselves and their families. Faculty alerted students who encountered academic difficulties, but process mapping revealed that the timing and steps taken by faculty varied, and students' expectations were rarely outlined. A unified intervention process that details both faculty members' and students' responsibilities for follow-up was needed. In addition, personal interactions and enhanced communication with students were other possible solutions to assist faculty identify and address the academic, clinical, and personal challenges that may impede students' success.

Implementing and Evaluating Solutions

From the beginning and throughout the PTR process, participating stakeholders offered solutions to address perceived problems. PTR leaders continuously reminded stakeholders that before solutions were developed, data needed to be collected and analyzed to better understand the contributing factors to admission, retention, and completion problems. Solutions needed to be based on evidence and focused on three areas: outreach, transitional support, and academic/clinical support.

Outreach.   Both survey responses and stakeholder feedback supported the need to improve the ADN program's visibility in the community and to increase outreach and education to populations who may be unaware of the nursing education opportunities available at Richland Community College. Based on the input of high school students and their guidance counselors, the PTR team developed a flyer and program banner to demonstrate the various paths students could take to become a registered nurse, including starting at a community college.

The team used these materials at various outreach activities with the goal of improving the diversity of the applicant pool and admitted cohort so that the students would reflect the college's racial-ethnic, age, and gender demographics. The team identified events where information could be disseminated to target student populations. For example, when the data revealed that a limited number of recent high school graduates were transitioning into and completing the degree, program staff and faculty sought opportunities to present information about the nursing program to high school students during college fairs, campus tours, classroom visits, and after-school programs.

Outreach was tracked by the number of events in which program faculty and staff participated. Data suggested that information was reaching the students who have, in the past, been underrepresented in the program. For example, African-American students represent approximately 15% of the Richland Community College's student body; however, between spring 2010 and spring 2012, African-American students made up only 10% of the students admitted to the ADN program. During the last four semesters, African-American students made up approximately 17% of admitted ADN students.

Data from ADN applicants revealed that Richland students relied heavily on other students preparing for program information. To ensure that correct information was delivered, program staff developed PASS 143 Introduction to Health Professions, a face-to-face workshop to assist current Richland students interested in health professions understand the selective admission process and terminology, create an academic plan, comprehend the expectations upon admission, and ask questions. Twenty-five students participated and evaluated PASS 143. The majority agreed that the workshop provided new information, addressed students' needs and questions, and was worth students' time.

Despite this positive start, only was section of PASS 143 enrolled more than five students in the Fall 2013. One student explained the workshop could be improved if more students took time to attend it but it was very informational. Several students felt more time was needed to cover the topics. Program faculty and staffs next steps are using this feedback, as well the responses from surveyed applicants, to design an online workshop that provides the information students seek in an easy-to-use format. How to incorporate faculty and student perspectives in this online platform is being considered.

Transitional Support.   To provide students with sufficient information to prepare for their transition to nursing, program staff developed PASS 141 Being a Successful Health Professions Student. This free, face-to-face workshop reviews program costs, financing options, financial responsibility, scheduling requirements, time management principles, goal setting, and academic and clinical expectations. The selected topics were based on faculty members' and students' input, as well as research that supports the need to teach time management skills and financial knowledge to incoming nursing students (Shelton, 2012; Williams, 2010).

A review of literature on nursing student retention also suggests that greater faculty support can have a positive impact on students' retention but requires faculty proactivity in approaching students who experience academic and personal difficulties (Shelton, 2012; Williams, 2010). According to Shelton (2012), students who feel they are part of a community are more likely to use available resources and persist in the academic program. To be proactive, to increase their personal interactions, and to integrate students to their new learning community, ADN faculty developed the "Meet Your Advisor" luncheon. Offered at the beginning of each semester, the luncheon provides an opportunity for new students to interact with their faculty advisors and current students, have their questions answered, and their fears dispelled.

Students who participated in the workshop and luncheon were asked to complete a short, optional survey about their experiences. Responses indicated that the majority of students agreed or strongly agreed that the activities provided new information, addressed students' questions, and were worth attending. Based on feedback from the applicant survey that suggested information be moved online, as well as to make best use of both students' and the presenters' time, program staff opted to move the workshop to an online learning platform for fall 2014. Although this was previously an optional workshop, students are now required to complete the online modules, submit assessments, and evaluate their experience.

New Directions for Community Colleges • DOI: 10.1002/cc

Surveys indicated that students like the online format and the opportunity to interact electronically with their future classmates. Program staff must continue to work towards incorporating faculty and current student perspectives in the online platform.

Prior to PTR, the ADN program experienced the highest attrition from first to second semester. From fall 2007 to spring 2012, the average first-to-second semester retention rate was 74.6%. Since implementing the free workshop and luncheon, the average first-to-second semester retention rate has increased to 89.2%.

Academic/Clinical Support.   The program's low completion rate also led faculty to discuss and identify ways to enhance communication with all students while also supporting their academic and clinical performance. Based on previous experience and a literature review, two faculty members proposed incorporating iPad technology to assist both students and faculty in locating medication information, accessing procedure videos, retrieving evidence-based practice articles, providing patient education, and documenting and communicating students' progress and clinical performance.

Faculty designed and administered a survey to measure students' and other faculty members' opinions about resources and communication at the clinical site before and after faculty had access to an iPad. Whereas access to needed resources and communication appeared to improve based on responses, it was evident that many faculty felt uncomfortable using the technology. More time and training was needed to find applications and tools that could help faculty improve student learning and assessment. It is unclear whether this technology has had a direct impact on retention and completion.

Lessons Learned

PTR challenged Richland's ADN faculty, staff, and stakeholders to consider the ways in which the program's processes were limiting access and completion for historically underserved student populations. To ensure that solutions were based on evidence, the PTR process required the college to analyze data, discuss inequities, map processes, and create program improvement and evaluation plans. As more community colleges seek to create a culture of evidence-based decision making, a process like PTR can help practitioners become more equity minded as they collect and analyze programs, processes, and student data. Colleges with a continuous improvement initiative in place can incorporate elements of PTR to ensure inequities in student outcomes are acknowledged, to ensure contributing factors to those inequities are identified, and to create and evaluate solutions.

Participation of institutional research (IR) professionals can help to develop equity-minded practitioners by providing training on quantitative and qualitative data collection, including disaggregation, and advising faculty and staff on how to create meaningful evaluation plans. During Richland's first PTR experience, the college did not have an IR staff member, therefore much of the program admission data collection and disaggregation required manual mining and plotting. The tools provided by OCCRL's PTR team were helpful, but to sustain the PTR work at Richland, faculty and staff needed access to IR staff who can help to determine effective data collection tools and develop adequate evaluation plans. For example, the iPad evaluation could have been more meaningful if the faculty had guidance from IR staff on how to formulate survey questions and collect data. IR staff who can respond to internal data requests are critical to a continuous improvement process focused on equity; unfortunately, IR staff are often overly consumed with external reporting requirements (Morest, 2009).

When college leaders are committed to improving career pathway programs such as Richland's ADN and addressing equity gaps, they can help to ensure that faculty and staff have the resources needed for data collection, analysis, experimentation, and innovation (Chaplot, Booth, & Johnstone, n.d.). Informing college leaders about the PTR team's work and experiences with the process is important to garnering their future support for program improvement projects that rely on the PTR or similar methodology. Richland highlighted the PTR team's work during statewide meetings, local radio shows, and a college board meeting.

Improving career pathway programs also requires the support of internal and external stakeholders. PTR helped Richland's ADN program establish relationships with various stakeholders who serve prospective students, in adult education, the workforce, and secondary education. As Richland seeks to transition more students from these various entry points into college, their continued input and assistance are required. Since completing the first PTR project, the college has had an opportunity to build on these relationships by completing a second PTR project, by developing an adult education health professions bridge program, and by identifying additional funding for low-income nursing students. This continued support helps both prospective and current students thrive.

Continuing improvements of the ADN program at Richland includes helping students to aspire to and access nursing through increased program marketing and recruitment; however, access and equity signify more than representative numbers in an applicant pool. The ADN program faculty and staff persist in improving retention and completion by continuing to examine student outcomes, analyze processes, evaluate and enhance current programs, and research and implement future initiatives that serve historically underrepresented and underserved student populations. There may be environmental factors affecting access and completion for which Richland cannot control, but for those factors that it can, the college is fortunate to have faculty and staff who continue to ask what more they can do to assist students to achieve their goals.

Statewide, PTR continues to grow. With new grants awarded in fall 2014, all but two community colleges have participated in the process, with countless secondary education and workforce, employer, and community partners engaged. A recent evaluation of PTR conducted by Alicia Dowd, codirector of CUE, found positive results, though there is room for improvement. Focus groups conducted by Dowd (personal communication, July 9, 2014) revealed that practitioners value PTR because they recognize that "the problem framing, data use, and decision-making processes structured by PTR are exactly the sort of analytical skills higher education professionals are expected to be able to demonstrate today" (p. 2). She also reported that PTR teams have uncovered and addressed inequities in student participation and outcomes, resulting in their wanting to know more about how to use data, how to secure better data, and how to share data-driven processes with others. These results are encouraging, but more needs to be done to address inequities that leave some student groups behind. Through continued efforts to implement and scale processes like PTR, there may be hope for improved educational experiences and outcomes for all learners.

References

Argyris, C. (1993). *On organizational learning.* Cambridge, MA: Blackwell.

Bathmaker, A. (2014, April). *The role of higher vocational pathways in enabling social mobility and supporting "vibrant" regional economies: an analysis of current trends and debates shaping English policy and practice.* Symposium presentation for the American Educational Research Association conference, Philadelphia, PA.

Bragg, D. (2014, April). *Career pathways in disparate industry sectors to serve underserved populations.* Symposium presentation for the American Educational Research Association conference, Philadelphia, PA.

Bragg, D., Dresser, L., & Smith, W. (2012). Leveraging workforce development and postsecondary education for low-skill, low-income workers: Lessons from the Shifting Gears Initiative. In L. A. Phelps (Ed.), *New Directions for Community Colleges: No. 157. Leveraging workforce development and postsecondary education for low-skill, low-income workers* (pp. 53–66). San Francisco, CA: Jossey-Bass.

Chaplot, P., Booth, K., & Johnstone, R. (n.d.). *Building a culture of inquiry: Using a cycle of exploring research and data to improve student success.* Retrieved from http://www.inquiry2improvement.com/attachments/article/12/CbD-Building.pdf

Denning, S. (2011). *The springboard: How storytelling ignites action in knowledge-era organizations.* Boston, MA: Butterworth-Heinemann.

Harmon, T., Liss, L., & Umbricht, M. (2012). *Process assessment* (Rev. ed.). Champaign, IL: Office of Community College Research and Leadership, University of Illinois at Urbana-Champaign. Retrieved from http://occrl.illinois.edu/files/Projects/ptr/Modules/PTR%20Module%203.pdf

Kanter, M., Ochoa, E., Nassif, R., & Chong, F. (2011, July). *Meeting President Obama's 2020 college completion goal* [PowerPoint Slides]. Retrieved from http://www.completionmatters.org/resource/meeting-president-obama%E2%80%99s-2020-college-completion-goal%0B

Morest, V. (2009). Accountability, accreditation, and continuous improvement: Building a culture of evidence. In C. Leimer (Ed.), *New Directions for Institutional Research: No. 143. Imagining the future of institutional research* (pp. 17–27). San Francisco, CA: Jossey-Bass.

Patton, M. (2011). *Developmental evaluation: Applying complexity concepts to enhance innovation and use.* New York, NY: Guilford Press.

Shelton, E. N. (2012). A model of nursing student retention. *International Journal of Nursing Education Scholarship, 9*(1), 1–16.

Wheelahan, L. (2014, April). *Rethinking pathways: Why a new approach is needed. A report from Australia.* Symposium presentation for the American Educational Research Association conference, Philadelphia, PA.

Williams, M. (2010). Attrition and retention in the nursing major: understanding persistence in beginning nursing students. *Nursing Education Perspective, 31*(6), 362–367.

JESSICA PICKEL is the director of adult education at Richland Community College. She served as the team leader for two Pathways to Results projects in her former role as the assistant to the dean.

DEBRA D. BRAGG is an Edward William Gutgsell and Jane Marr Gutgsell Endowed Professor and director of the Office of Community College Research and Leadership at the University of Illinois at Urbana-Champaign.

NEW DIRECTIONS FOR COMMUNITY COLLEGES • DOI: 10.1002/cc

5

Many community colleges are unwelcoming to LGBTQ students and this chapter provides practical suggestions to community college leaders to develop a more inclusive campus culture.

Call to Action: Embracing an Inclusive LGBTQ Culture on Community College Campuses

Jason L. Taylor

In March 2014, a transgender student at Central Piedmont Community College was leaving the women's restroom when she was stopped by a campus police officer and asked to show her identification. The student, Andraya Williams, claimed that campus police detained her and embarrassed her for a reason unbeknownst to her. Central Piedmont claimed that the officer believed Williams was a man dressed as a woman going into the women's restroom. Ultimately, campus police officers escorted Williams off campus, but Williams was allowed to return to class the next day.[1]

This incident, which garnered attention and coverage in the national media, is one of many incidents that lesbian, gay, bisexual, transgender, and queer (LGBTQ) students encounter on a regular basis on community college campuses. Unlike this incident, however, many incidents go unreported, and as a result, LGBTQ students' safety and security are threatened as they pursue their postsecondary pathways.

Williams' narrative is not unfamiliar, however, because the reality is that some students report these incidents, and colleges and universities often struggle to understand LGBTQ students' concerns and appropriately respond to these concerns. In the best-case scenario, students such as Williams challenge institutional practices and the laissez-faire institutional approach to LGBTQ student needs, and students persevere toward their educational goals with minimal emotional and psychological harm. In the worst-case scenario, institutional and cultural norms prevail and students take their own life, as was the tragic case when Tyler Clementi took his life on the Rutgers University campus in 2010 (Stripling, 2010). The fact

New Directions for Community Colleges, no. 172, Winter 2015 © 2015 Wiley Periodicals, Inc.
Published online in Wiley Online Library (wileyonlinelibrary.com) • DOI: 10.1002/cc.20163

that Clementi's roommate felt it was acceptable to video record Clementi with his same-sex partner and publish it online in a Rutgers dorm room is a partial reflection of the institutional culture that would promote or not condemn such behavior. Although Clementi's roommate's behavior may not be representative of all heterosexual students, this type of student behavior should signal to all institutions of higher education that homophobic and heterosexist attitudes and behaviors may be embedded in college campus cultures, inside and outside of the classroom.

These incidents and others surface several facts that community college leaders and administrators must address. First, although we do not have data on the representation of LGBTQ students on community college campuses, it is likely that LGBTQ students are enrolled in most institutions of higher education across the country. Yet many institutions have not changed institutional policy and culture to reflect this fact. Second, it is not just that LGBTQ students are enrolled in most community colleges, but these students are often visible and active members of campus communities or the larger community. Third, I highlighted the Williams incident in this chapter because most efforts to improve the campus climate and experience for LGBTQ students are concentrated at universities and 4-year colleges and *not* at community colleges.

To illustrate the latter point, Campus Pride's 2014 list of the 50 best LGBT-friendly colleges and universities does not include a single community college.[2] Further, Campus Pride's full index of 427 colleges and universities that have "demonstrated an active interest in LGBT issues and an ongoing commitment to LGBT & Ally people" includes only 37 community colleges (Campus Pride, 2014, n.p.). Despite the fact that community colleges enroll 45% of all undergraduates in the United States (American Association of Community Colleges, 2014), they represent only 9% of the institutions that have demonstrated some form of explicit commitment to being LGBT-friendly according to the Campus Pride Index.

With this in mind, my goal with this chapter is twofold: (a) to illustrate why community colleges should care about and support LGBTQ students; and (b) to articulate how community colleges can take action to change institutional policy and practice to become more LGBTQ friendly and, more important, ensure that *all* students are successful.

The Social and Policy Context

It is important for community colleges leaders to understand LGBTQ students' experiences in the larger social and cultural context within the United States. It is no secret that there are systematic biases against LGBTQ people in the United States as evidenced by public policies that fail to protect and support LGBTQ people in our social and cultural institutions. For example, it is legal for employers in many states to fire LGBTQ people solely due to their sexual orientation or gender identity, and the United

NEW DIRECTIONS FOR COMMUNITY COLLEGES • DOI: 10.1002/cc

States Congress has failed to pass antidiscrimination laws to protect LGBTQ citizens in the workplace. Another harmful policy was the U.S. military's Don't Ask Don't Tell policy that was fortunately revoked in 2012. Similarly, the U.S. Supreme Court ruled the Defense of Marriage Act unconstitutional in summer 2014 and overturned lower court rulings in *Obergefell v. Hodges* in summer 2015. These rulings reversed decades of legal discrimination, which restricted access to basic rights for LGBTQ couples—for example, financial and economic privileges, access to high-quality health care, and parenting rights and privileges. We also see evidence of discrimination against LGBTQ people in health care policies such as the U.S. Department of Health and Human Services' policy that bans blood, tissue, and organ donations from men who report having sex with other men (Cray, 2012). Even as some national policies improve for LGBTQ people, the negative effects of the policies may persist and the weight of those policies may be shouldered by LGBTQ people for years after harmful policies are reversed.

Despite one's political persuasion on public policies affecting LGBTQ people, the fact remains that the discriminatory effects of policies have a negative impact on LGBTQ people resulting in perceptions of stigma (Pew Research Center, 2013) and adverse health outcomes (Hatzenbuehler, 2010). It is critical that community college faculty, staff, and administrators understand this larger social context because it is within this context that many LGBTQ students experience and understand their identity. Students bring these experiences and perceptions with them when they enroll in community college classes, interact with peers in study groups and clubs, and engage with faculty and staff.

Homophobia and Heterosexism.   A useful way to understand this larger social and cultural context is to understand what shapes cultural attitudes and beliefs. Homophobia and heterosexism are two dominant forces that influence equity for LGBTQ communities. Homophobia refers to fear of or discrimination against homosexuality or homosexual individuals. Heterosexism has a similar definition and is sometimes preferred over homophobia because it "highlights the parallels between antigay sentiment and other forms of prejudice, such as racism, anti-Semitism, and sexism" (Herek, 2014, n.p.); I use heterosexism for the remainder of the chapter. Herek (1996) contends that heterosexism operates at both the individual level and the cultural level. Heterosexism at the individual level includes "personal disgust, hostility, or condemnation of homosexuality" (p. 102). At the cultural level, heterosexism is pervasive in our social institutions and evident in noninclusive hate laws, lack of domestic partnership benefits, the only recent inclusion of LGBTQ people in marriage laws, and other associated norms and regulations that exclude or discriminate against LGBTQ individuals (Herek, 1996). It is also important to recognize that heterosexism is not always intentional and can manifest itself in our innocuous everyday actions, behaviors, and assumptions.

NEW DIRECTIONS FOR COMMUNITY COLLEGES • DOI: 10.1002/cc

Heterosexism on College Campuses.   The pervasiveness of hetero-sexism on college campuses provides a compelling case for why community college campuses need to better support LGBTQ students. Heterosexism manifests itself in many ways on college campuses and research on students can be organized into at least two categories: (a) the perceptions, attitudes, and behaviors of heterosexual students, and (b) the perceptions and experiences of LGBTQ students. Because we have little research on LGBTQ students in the community college context (Leider, 2012; Zamani-Gallaher & Choudhuri, 2011), the vast majority of the research and empirical evidence is based on the 4-year context.

Researchers have studied and documented heterosexual students' attitudes and perceptions of LGBTQ students on college campuses. For example, D'Augelli and Rose (1990) studied the attitudes of a sample of heterosexual students at one university. The majority of participants in their study reported that homosexuality was disgusting and/or wrong and believed that LGBTQ students would be exposed to harassment. Malaney, Williams, and Geller (1997) studied students at two institutions and reported that 60% of students knew heterosexual students who made antihomosexual comments. These studies and several others surface the deeply engrained heterosexist climate that permeates many college campuses.

This hostile and negative climate toward LGBTQ students is also evidenced by the perceptions and experiences of LGBTQ students on college campuses. Research from single institutional studies (e.g., D'Augelli, 1989; Rhoads, 1994; Tetreault, Fette, Meidlinger, & Hope, 2013) and multi-institutional studies (e.g., Rankin, 2003; Rankin, Blumenfeld, Weber, & Frazer, 2010) leads to similar conclusions: The majority of LGBTQ students experience harassment in some form (verbal, physical, and vandalism) and often perceive the campus climate to be hostile and unwelcoming. Research also documents that LGBTQ college students are more likely than their heterosexual peers to have seriously considered attempting suicide (Kisch, Leino, & Silverman, 2005). Collectively, these studies and other research suggest that college campuses are unwelcoming and hostile toward LGBTQ students, and they also suggest that campus leaders have not done enough to prevent these negative experiences and create a more inclusive environment for LGBTQ students.

The few empirical studies that have examined the intersection of community colleges and LGBTQ students confirms some of what is known from the 4-year context. For example, in a survey of undergraduate students, Franklin (1998) reported widespread incidence of heterosexism. Similarly, more recent research found that classroom environments are not welcoming (Nelson, 2010), the classroom environment is a strong predictor of LGBTQ students' overall perceptions of campus climate (Garvey, Taylor, & Rankin, 2014), and resources and programming for LGBTQ students are mostly absent on community college campuses (Manning, Pring, & Glider, 2012).

NEW DIRECTIONS FOR COMMUNITY COLLEGES • DOI: 10.1002/cc

Toward Inclusivity in Community Colleges

As previously mentioned, the dearth of research on LGBTQ community college students leaves much to be desired, and it is difficult to provide research-based recommendations in the community college context. However, drawing from the research on 4-year institutions and a few studies on LGBTQ community college students, there are practical and reasonable changes in policy and practice that community colleges can embrace in order to move toward a more inclusive campus environment for LGBTQ community college students. Next, I provide five recommendations that community college leaders should implement, as a starting point, to improve the campus climate for LGBTQ students.

Institutional Commitment.   Arguably the most important action needed by community colleges is an institutional commitment to support LGBTQ students, as well as equity-minded leadership (as discussed by Felix et al., Chapter 3). The prospects of the other recommendations in this chapter ultimately rest on the will and capacity of leaders to elevate LGBTQ students and issues to the campus level. Leaders must be intentional and strategic about how to engage this issue on campus, particularly if there is resistance from a local board of trustees or from faculty and staff. The reality is that LGBTQ issues are sometimes politically unpopular, uncomfortable, and difficult issues to discuss, and in some conservative communities there may not be an appetite to discuss, let alone act, on LGBTQ issues.

Although efforts to support LGBTQ students on many community college campuses have been bottom up and not top down, the commitment of institutional leadership sends a clear signal to the campus community and has the potential to ensure the long-term success of efforts to support LGBTQ students. To begin, community college leaders can create a task force on LGBTQ student success. A task force or working group can serve as the launching pad for the recommendations that follow. Similarly, a letter or statement by the president announcing institutional efforts and actions signals to students, faculty, and staff that the institution is committed to supporting LGBTQ students. It is also critical to recognize that any institutional efforts to support LGBTQ students will need fiscal resources to support new initiatives, staff time, or other resources, so it is important that leaders are willing to commit financial resources to the task force.

Climate Survey and Needs Assessment.   Many colleges and universities have conducted institutional surveys to assess the campus climate, experiences, and needs of their LGBTQ students. Sue Rankin and her colleagues have pioneered some of this work over the past decade at the institutional level and nationally (Rankin et al., 2010). A survey provides the community college with a benchmark or baseline to help the college understand basic information about their LGBTQ students including an estimate of the number and proportion of LGBTQ students on campus, the extent to which LGBTQ students perceive the campus as welcoming and

NEW DIRECTIONS FOR COMMUNITY COLLEGES • DOI: 10.1002/cc

safe, LGBTQ students' experiences in and out of the classroom, and, most important, the needs of LGBTQ students. The survey data provide an evidence base for institutional recommendations and action to support LGBTQ students. Community college leaders can visit the Campus Pride website to read the executive summary of Rankin et al.'s (2010) national campus climate survey to better understand what information a survey might provide their institution.[3]

In addition to providing timely and useful information to community college leaders, a survey has the potential to raise the institutional consciousness about LGBTQ students and issues that might otherwise be muted. One logical explanation for the absence of institutional efforts to support LGBTQ students is general lack of awareness not only about LGBTQ students and issues but also about the relationship between LGBTQ students' experiences and their potential academic success. Many faculty and staff may not know there are LGBTQ students on campus, let alone students' concerns and perspectives regarding campus climate. Student voices and input are valuable and can be a powerful catalyst for action and change.

Faculty and Staff Training and Development.   Research and institutional practice suggest that a key need for higher education institutions is to provide training and development to faculty and staff. Heterosexist attitudes and beliefs are often embedded in the everyday actions of community college faculty, staff, and students whether intentional or not (i.e., the Williams story at the beginning of this chapter), and training about how to identify and mitigate heterosexism is a practical starting point for faculty and staff. One common strategy is to implement Ally or Safe Zone training, which are often one-time workshops that cover a range of topics relevant to LGBTQ students and people. After participation, faculty and staff receive a pink triangle to display on their office door that signals to students that the individual's office is a safe and welcoming space (often called a Safe Zone). Safe Zones are an important signal to LGBTQ students given that research shows many students feel unsafe on campus. One criticism of Ally and Safe Zone programs is that they are optional for faculty and staff, so the reach of such programs mostly extends to those who wish to participate. Although an important audience for training and development, those individuals with a propensity to support LGBTQ students are likely not the group perpetuating heterosexism on campus.

A key leverage point for training and development is the curriculum and classroom, as research suggests that the classroom climate is a significant predictor of students' overall perceptions of campus climate in community colleges (Garvey, Taylor, & Rankin, 2014). Students also report that heterosexist comments are not challenged by faculty, and in some cases, perpetuated by faculty. Faculty may make heteronormative assumptions when discussing topics in class or during class activities, and they may fail to integrate LGBTQ topics and authors in the curriculum. Faculty bring their own biases and perceptions into the classroom, which should be expected of any faculty member, but it is problematic when these biases negatively influence students' learning and development. Faculty training on the use of heteronormative assumptions and language is one solution to address this problem, but another is to develop an LGBTQ curriculum and teaching assessment that allow faculty to assess their own curriculum and pedagogy to determine the extent to which it is inclusive. Although we have few examples of this in higher education, the health education community has generated resources[4] as has the Gay, Lesbian, & Straight Education Network (GLSEN) at the K–12 level.[5]

Peer Outreach and Leadership.   Research suggests that peer-to-peer engagement on LGBTQ issues between LGBTQ and heterosexual students can decrease heterosexist attitudes toward LGBTQ people among heterosexual students (Nelson & Krieger, 1997). Many university and 4-year campuses deliver panel presentations or peer presentations about LGBTQ people and students in an effort to directly engage heterosexual students with queer issues. Although these types of outreach may have positive benefits, this type of programming requires active student leaders and may place undue burden on LGBTQ students. Further, voluntary attendance at events will likely not reach all students or reach the students who arguably have the most to benefit from the peer engagement. That said, student affairs could be strategic about integrating peer and panel presentations into regular student programming events. Also, community college faculty teaching general education courses in the social sciences or humanities could integrate peer presentations into their curriculum where appropriate, given that the majority of students take general education courses.

Campus Resources and Policies.   Although much work remains to be done on many college and university campuses across the country, significant progress has been made to create LGBTQ resource centers and hire full-time and/or part-time professional support staff for LGBTQ students, greatly expanding professional expertise on college campuses. According to the Consortium of Higher Education LGBT Resource Professionals website, there were almost 600 members in 2013, which represents almost a 100% increase from 2007. It is unclear how many of these members represent community colleges, but given the relatively small number of community colleges on the Campus Pride Index, it is unlikely that many community colleges have professional support for LGBTQ students who are active in the consortium. Creating an inclusive climate and culture on community college campuses is no small feat, and community colleges would benefit by investing in a full-time and/or part-time staff person to coordinate this work and support LGBTQ students. Indeed, many 4-year colleges and universities have adopted this strategy as the LGBTQ resource center director often is responsible for a wide range of tasks that include programming for campus-wide LGBTQ events, advising student groups, consulting campus units, representing the LGBTQ perspective on committees, and others. The creation of a LGBTQ resource center and director also serves as a tangible and visible commitment by the community college to support LGBTQ students. Further, and arguably most important, a center and director bring professional expertise to an issue that is worthy of such attention and expertise.

Finally, community college leaders can analyze existing campus policies. Relatively simple policy changes can be quite meaningful to LGBTQ students. For example, expanding nondiscrimination statements to include LGBTQ identities sends an important signal to students that the community college does not tolerate discrimination based on sexual orientation and gender identity. Similarly, establishing gender-neutral restroom facilities and related policies are relatively simple immediate actions. Other policy changes, such as policies on faculty and staff training requirements or curriculum inclusivity, may need to emerge from the ground up based on institutional assessments and collaboration.

Final Thoughts

Although it appears that much work remains to be done in community colleges to support LGBTQ students, existing practices in 4-year colleges and universities provide useful models for program and policy development and implementation; community colleges do not need to reinvent the wheel. Given that community college students represent 45% of the undergraduate population, it is imperative that community colleges respond to this call to action and leverage their resources to engage and support LGBTQ students. Incidents such as the Williams case should serve as important signals to community colleges about the need to address systemic bias in the form of homophobia and heterosexism. The recommendations outlined in this chapter are a starting point for community colleges to change institutional and cultural norms that often tolerate and perpetuate heterosexism and ultimately have a negative impact on LGBTQ students. These recommendations are not intended to simply appease LGBTQ students or quell LGBTQ concerns, but they are also intended to address entrenched systematic biases and have the potential to improve conditions for LGBTQ students and communities.

It is unlikely that LGBTQ student concerns are going away any time soon. Social policy changes and public attitudes toward LGBTQ people are shifting in the United States, and LGBTQ individuals feeling more supported, legitimized, and empowered. This changing social tide will undoubtedly spill into institutions of higher education, and community colleges have an opportunity now to better support LGBTQ students' emotional, psychological, physical, and academic well-being and success.

Notes

1. See   https://www.insidehighered.com/news/2014/04/02/debate-central-piedmont
-over-transgender-student-rights

2. See http://www.campuspride.org/resources/2014top50lgbt-friendlycolleges/

NEW DIRECTIONS FOR COMMUNITY COLLEGES • DOI: 10.1002/cc

3. See http://www.campuspride.org/research/projects-publications/
4. See http://www.lgbthealtheducation.org/
5. See http://www.glsen.org/educate/resources/curriculum

References

American Association of Community College. (2014). *2014 fact sheet*. Washington, DC: Author.

Campus Pride. (2014). *LGBT-Friendly Campus Pride Index*. Retrieved from http://www.campusprideindex.com

Cray, A. (2012). *Discriminatory donor policies substitute stereotypes for science*. Washington, DC: Center for American Progress. Retrieved from http://www.americanprogress.org/issues/lgbt/news/2012/09/11/37294/discriminatory-donor-policies-substitute-stereotypes-for-science/

D'Augelli, A. (1989). Homophobia in a university community: Views of prospective resident assistants. *Journal of College Student Development, 30*(6), 546–552.

D'Augelli, A., & Rose, M. (1990). Homophobia in a university community: Attitudes and experiences of heterosexual freshmen. *Journal of College Student Development, 31*(6), 484–491.

Franklin, K. (1998, May). *Psychological motivations of hate crimes perpetrators: Implications for educational intervention*. Paper presented at the 106th Annual Convention of the American Psychological Association, San Francisco, CA.

Garvey, J., Taylor, J. L., & Rankin, S. (2014). An examination of campus climate for LGBTQ community college students. *Community College Journal of Research and Practice, 39*, 527–541.

Hatzenbuehler, M. I. (2010). Social factors as determinants of mental health disparities in LGB populations: Implications for public policy. *Social Issues and Policy Review, 4*(1), 31–62.

Herek, G. M. (1996). Heterosexism and homophobia. In R. P. Cabaj & T. S. Stein (Eds.), *Textbook of homosexuality and mental health* (pp. 101–113). Washington, DC: American Psychiatric Press.

Herek, G. M. (2014). *Definitions: Homophobia, heterosexism, and sexual prejudice*. Retrieved from http://psychology.ucdavis.edu/faculty_sites/rainbow/html/prej_defn.html

Kisch, J., Leino, E. V., & Silverman, M. M. (2005). Aspects of suicide behavior, depression, and treatment in college students: Results from the Spring 2000 National College Health Assessment Survey. *Suicide and Life-Threatening Behavior, 35*, 3–13.

Leider, S. J. (2012). LGBTQ people on community college campuses: A 20-year review. *Community College Journal of Research and Practice, 37*(7), 471–474.

Malaney, G. D., Williams, E. A., & Geller, W. W. (1997). Assessing campus climate for gays, lesbians, and bisexuals at two institutions. *Journal of College Student Development, 38*, 365–375.

Manning, P., Pring, L., & Glider, P. (2012). Relevance of campus climate for alcohol and other drug use among LGBTQ community college students: A statewide qualitative assessment. *Community College Journal of Research and Practice, 36*(7), 494–503.

Nelson, C. D. (2010). A gay immigrant student's perspective: Unspeakable acts in the language class. *TESOL Quarterly, 44*(3), 441–464.

Nelson, E. S., & Krieger, S. L. (1997). Changes in attitudes toward homosexuality in college students: Implementation of a gay men and lesbian peer panel. *Journal of Homosexuality, 33*(2), 63–81.

Pew Research Center. (2013). *A survey of LGBT Americans: Attitudes, experiences and values in changing times*. Retrieved from http://www.pewsocialtrends.org/files/2013/06/SDT_LGBT-Americans_06-2013.pdf

Rankin, S. (2003). *Campus climate for gay, lesbian, bisexual, and transgender people: A national perspective.* Cambridge, MA: The Policy Institute of the National Gay and Lesbian Task Force.

Rankin, S., Blumenfeld, W. J., Weber, G. N., & Frazer, S. (2010). *State of higher education for LGBT people.* Charlotte, NC: Campus Pride.

Rhoads, R. A. (1994). Implications of the growing visibility of gay and bisexual male students on campus. *NASPA Journal, 34,* 67–74.

Stripling, J. (2010, October 1). *Deadly warning.* Retrieved from https://www.inside highered.com/news/2010/10/01/rutgers

Tetreault, P. A., Fette, R., Meidlinger, P. C., & Hope, D. (2013). Perceptions of campus climate by sexual minorities. *Journal of Homosexuality, 70*(7), 947–964.

Zamani-Gallaher, E. M., & Choudhuri, D. D. (2011). A primer on LGBTQ students at community colleges: Considerations for research and practice. In E. M. Cox & J. S. Watson (Eds.), *New Directions for Community Colleges: No. 155. Marginalized students* (pp. 35–49). San Francisco, CA: Jossey-Bass.

JASON L. TAYLOR *is an assistant professor in the Department of Educational Leadership and Policy at the University of Utah.*

6

This chapter argues that, despite intentions, the way federal financial aid policy is constructed and currently administered can have negative consequences for poor community college students.

Do Financial Aid Policies Unintentionally Punish the Poor, and What Can We Do About It?

Courtney A. Campbell, Regina Deil-Amen, Cecilia Rios-Aguilar

Important equity concerns exist regarding federal financial aid policy and its implementation in community college contexts because of procedural impediments and a *climate of penalty* imposed on students and financial aid staff. Aid policies do a disservice to this already underresourced higher education sector when the implementation, oversight, and policing of federal financial aid create overwhelming inefficiencies that can harm the success of students who need this aid most. Despite recent efforts to streamline the FAFSA (Free Application for Federal Student Aid), accessing and processing federal financial aid remains burdensome for many community college students who can face additional hurdles and fear, which in turn create stress for students and an increased workload for already understaffed institutions. Originally, the Pell grant program, a part of federal financial aid, was designed to assist students from low-income families by providing an equal opportunity to attend college relative to their peers from higher income families. However, as an increasing percentage of the cost of college attendance shifts to the student as state revenues decrease, the Pell grant program is in a perilous position. Increased operating costs and questions about its ability to effectively cover the costs of college place the program in a vulnerable position. Numerous proposals are trying to "fix" the program by improving small-scale efficiencies, but they pay little attention to broader, large-scale efforts to ensure the continued effectiveness of the program in facilitating college access (Baime & Mullin, 2011).

Students attending 2-year institutions are often considered nontraditional students. According to the College Board (2013), 36% of all Pell

New Directions for Community Colleges, no. 172, Winter 2015 © 2015 Wiley Periodicals, Inc.
Published online in Wiley Online Library (wileyonlinelibrary.com) • DOI: 10.1002/cc.20164

grant recipients were attending public 2-year colleges in 2011–2012. About a quarter of all recipients at 2-year colleges were 31 years old and older, and 38% were independent students with their own dependents. Nearly 80% of recipients at 2-year colleges have family incomes of less than 150% of the federal poverty threshold, meaning that the average income for a family of four is $35,775, so exploring how aid is accessed and used at these institutions is critical to understanding the role of federal financial aid in serving high-poverty student populations (Baime & Mullin, 2011). Questions of equity surrounding federal financial aid for community college students tend to focus on improving students' awareness and use of available financial aid (Advisory Committee on Student Financial Assistance, 2008). These efforts stem from the understanding that the receipt of federal financial aid, particularly need-based grants like the Pell grant program, positively affects student persistence (McKinney & Novak, 2013; Mendoza, Mendez, & Malcolm, 2009). Accordingly, federal financial aid reform has revolved around the streamlining and simplification of the FAFSA application process in an effort to increase the number of students submitting annual applications (Bettinger, Long, Oreopoulos, & Sanbonmatsu, 2012). Although these efforts are important, our research reveals an aspect of the process that has been neglected by both reformers and researchers: the excessive procedural demands community colleges face related to student aid eligibility and disbursement *after* the initial FAFSA application process.

In this chapter we argue that, despite intentions, the way federal financial aid policy, including the Pell grant program, is constructed and currently administered can have negative consequences for poor students and the institutions in which they are highly concentrated—community colleges. The policies and their implementation fuel what we call a *climate of penalty*, where various punitive measures are levied against students and dominate their experience of financial aid. Furthermore, we examine what happens with financial aid for community college students on an ongoing basis postenrollment. Using interviews and posts from a social media application, we consider the challenges that students experience in receiving their federal financial aid, including receiving funds in a timely fashion and understanding and navigating policies and procedures, and the potential that these policies and procedures have to aggravate inequity.

Schools App and Student Interviews

Schools App is a mobile/web-based social media platform designed for current and newly admitted students to interact with each other exclusively within their own college community. The application is Facebook based and internal to each college, for use only by invited students, staff, faculty, and administrators. By posting and commenting on the app, students create a community marked mainly by the asking of questions, the seeking and

NEW DIRECTIONS FOR COMMUNITY COLLEGES • DOI: 10.1002/cc

offering of advice and information, and the sharing of interests and academic experiences. Some staff maintain a consistent presence on the app in order to answer questions, provide information, post, and observe posts. The various interactions that take place through the app make it a unique site of investigation, particularly because financial aid emerged as a frequent topic in student posts. We used the app to understand the climate and culture of financial aid at eight different community colleges across eight different states.

We examined data from two primary sources: (a) the text data collected from the "school feed" of the app since adoption of the application in fall 2011, and (b) data from interviews and focus groups conducted with nearly 800 students and staff members in 2012 and 2013. The schools in our sample had student populations receiving Pell from 21% at the most rural school to 48%. Interviews were analyzed using a grounded approach with open coding. All posts from 2011 through 2013 were analyzed by first generating word clouds to identify the most frequently used words then returning to the posts and using open coding to determine how and in what context the words were used. From multiple analyses of over 92,000 posts, we learned that financial aid was one of the most prominent topics on the app, despite the fact that the app was never intended for this purpose. As stated before, it was primarily intended to build community. Instead, students defined the app as a space to reach out for help with financial aid questions and dilemmas. The app data provided a window into how and when students had questions about the financial aid process or were experiencing challenges, and the interviews gave us an opportunity to learn more about the obstacles and frustrations financial aid seemed to pose, as well as students' strategies for navigating them.

Financial Aid: The Student Experience

Student posts and comments on the app reveal the questions they have and the challenges they face relevant to federal financial aid. The app exchanges provide visible data on how students experience federal financial aid procedures and policies, exposing inequities that may otherwise go unnoticed but might be more prevalent for students clustered in community colleges, particularly students who do not fit the traditional mold. It is unfair to both community colleges and their students if federal policies foster practices that may be creating inequities. By examining the content of these social media exchanges and the experiences students shared in their interviews, we are able to better understand how federal financial aid might be having unintended consequences that work against the goal of equity. The purpose of federal financial aid policies is, presumably, to maximize program impact and minimize the waste of federal tax dollars. However, the associated policies and rules with federal financial aid create additional hoops and complications for students, which can ultimately penalize them and create a punitive climate for those struggling to navigate requirements and procedures. As students engage in conversations about financial aid through interviews and posts on social media, the difficulties they encounter and stress they experience are illuminated. Federal financial aid policies that are intended to streamline services can create an atmosphere where students' strengths, efforts, and successes are unacknowledged while policing efforts are used to reduce or prevent aid infractions or identify those unworthy of aid. Through our research, we identified two main challenges that students face in accessing federal financial aid: delays in disbursement and procedural and eligibility issues.

Delays in Disbursement.   First-year undergraduate students receiving their first federal loan must wait 30 days from the start of the semester to collect loan money as a stipulation of federal financial aid. At some institutions, students must wait 30 days for their Pell grant disbursement as well. Students posting on the app continuously question if and when they will receive their financial aid, particularly those waiting to receive a "refund" of their Pell grant after tuition is paid. The ambiguity of the federal financial aid process and disbursement dates causes strain on students who depend upon their aid for rent, transportation, and other living expenses. Thus, students who begin the semester without access to their "refund" money face scarcity and uncertainty, especially those who have reduced their income and work hours or who need to pay for childcare to successfully manage their college enrollment. Posts and exchanges on the app suggest that students experience the delay in disbursement as unnecessarily punitive, especially given that they are serious students struggling and sacrificing to attend college.

Some community colleges have instituted policies that purposely delay federal aid disbursement in order to prevent what college staff described in interviews as "Pell runners," students who accept financial aid dollars but do not attend class for the rest of the semester in order to earn money. Although colleges generally experience a loss of students at the beginning of each semester, no systematic research has shown if or how many students are actually intentionally abusing the system. Moreover, ambiguity exists regarding the extent to which systemic forces that create challenges for students, such as poverty, influence students in their ability to persist in the beginning of the semester. However, it appears that federal financial aid policies, like the 30-day waiting period, are based on the unfounded assumption that students are widely abusing this privilege. This form of policing elicits complaints from students who experience stress from delayed disbursement. App posts reveal students feel that they are being punished for the actions of others because they cannot have ready access to their money to use it for what it is intended—books, materials, and college-relevant living expenses. In reality, community college students are penalized because their institutions serve a majority of students who, because of poverty and related environmental circumstances, are targeted as abusers of the system.

NEW DIRECTIONS FOR COMMUNITY COLLEGES • DOI: 10.1002/cc

Delays in financial aid disbursement also occur for other reasons ranging from application errors to holdups in processing paperwork or money. Financial aid offices are often overwhelmed, with few staff members processing thousands of students. This is especially problematic when many students applying for and receiving federal financial aid at each college do not fit the traditional family structure for which financial aid policies were designed. At community college campuses where the financial aid office has a presence on the app, staff are able to communicate information about eligibility criteria, overrides, and delays or upcoming disbursement dates to students. The app enables staff and researchers to see what students experience as they voice their distress concerning if and when they will receive their financial aid. At several colleges, staff provide answers to questions directly on the app unless confidential information is involved, in which case staff often encourage students to e-mail or call them directly. These financial aid advisors and related staff are faced with extraordinary burdens in terms of student frustration and criticism due to delays experienced by students. However, these delays are typically not the fault of those working directly with students. They are a result of system design based on larger structural and policy inequities, and they produce a negative climate for both students and staff trying to adapt and maneuver, given the policies.

In interviews and through app exchanges, students describe how delays in disbursement affect their academics, especially when they cannot readily purchase books and supplies necessary for class. Their inability to purchase materials leaves low-income students without the same resources as their peers, who can afford to pay for books and supplies out of pocket. Some community colleges in the study address this gap by providing students with a debit card to use prior to federal financial aid disbursement. The debit card allows students to purchase supplies, but they are unable to purchase anything outside of the campus bookstore (which is often the most expensive option), forcing students to spend more of their financial aid dollars on books than is necessary. As a result, some students begin the semester without books and supplies, hoping that their financial aid comes through soon. The app highlights student concerns about starting the semester without necessary supplies, fearing they will be unable to keep up with their classes without access to books and supplies required by instructors.

Procedural and Eligibility Issues. Community college students' divergence from the federally defined "dependent/independent" criteria for financial aid places them at a disadvantage in terms of eligibility. Students can request a change from dependent to independent status only if they can document extreme, unique, or unusual family circumstances such as abuse, neglect, or parental desertion. The burden of proof is on the student to document that their family form is "abnormal" in order to receive additional funding to finance their college attendance. As a result, busy community college aid officers become overburdened by cases with special circumstances that must be considered on a case-by-case basis. This further stretches an already limited staff and further complicates the federal financial aid process for already financially struggling students.

Students receive federal financial aid proportional to their course load, with full-time students eligible to receive more money than those attending part time. App users occasionally express concern about their semester plans when they are not sure how much financial aid money to expect. Students who use federal financial aid for living expenses are especially vulnerable if their aid amount fluctuates from year to year. Students often must take their financial aid package into consideration when choosing what and how many classes to take, even if it is detrimental to their academic success or prolongs their enrollment. Many students do not withdraw from or drop classes in which they are doing poorly because they do not want to lose or waste their aid. This behavior can, in turn, have a negative effect on their grade point average (GPA), which influences their overall aid eligibility. Students not dependent on federal financial aid have the freedom to drop or withdraw from classes in which they are doing poorly without worrying whether dropping that class will affect their ability to pay for college. These students do not have to make choices between potentially sacrificing their GPA by remaining in classes in which they are not doing well and losing their means of paying for college.

Additionally, some students address the impact of the maximum time limit requirement on their eligibility. Federal financial aid, both through the disbursement of student loans and Pell grants, include "maximum eligibility" restrictions, which dictate the amount of funds one may receive over a lifetime and is "limited by federal law to be the equivalent of six years of Pell grant funding" (U.S. Department of Education, 2014). Students fear losing their aid if they do not pursue an efficient enough path through postsecondary education. This is particularly problematic for students who must first complete developmental coursework, those who attempt college at multiple institutions (some beginning at for-profits) before degree completion, and for those who transfer after accumulating more credit than will officially be accepted toward their 4-year degree program of choice. Because students dependent on financial aid often plan their lives and coursework around financial aid, the unpredictability of their award amount, their heavy reliance on full financial aid award, and their preoccupation with losing their aid can be problematic, increasing inequity by hindering a student's ability to succeed.

Students receiving Pell grants must make Satisfactory Academic Progress (SAP) to remain Pell eligible. Guidelines set by each institution generally include requirements such as maintaining a 2.0 or above GPA, as well as completing a certain percentage of the classes a student enrolls in each semester as a measure of adequate progress. Many of the Pell grant recipients we interviewed dipped below a 2.0 at one time in their past academic history. Maintaining financial aid eligibility is a major source of stress for community college students, who are among those most likely to be dealing with poverty, financial instability, and related life crises—all of which can, at any point, threaten their academic performance and, consequently, their ability to continue in college due to the loss of their financial aid eligibility. Many of the students we interviewed lived in fear of such peril or had suffered from loss of aid due to their academic struggles. Many had lost financial aid due to a low GPA (possibly initially caused by difficulties with financial aid) and were struggling to regain eligibility, whereas others were attempting to maintain the delicate balance between minimum credits they must take to be eligible for financial aid and becoming overloaded with coursework. Students who are unable to maintain a balance may end up sacrificing their financial aid eligibility. One semester where life interferes with school may mean financial aid eligibility probation or a temporary loss of their financial aid, further complicating their attempts to continue their education. Students feel pressure to continue taking and passing courses in which they are struggling in order to avoid financial aid penalties, even when life circumstances, such as family death, illness, or job loss, become overwhelming.

Recommendations for Action

Although the federal financial aid system was created with the idea of determining the financial need of recent high school graduates who are dependent on their parents and attend college full time, community college students are a diverse group and do not fit this model. Most community college students are considered "neo-traditional" (Long, 2010, p. 53), meaning that they are likely to delay enrollment after high school, work full time while enrolled, be financially independent, have dependents other than a spouse, receive public assistance, or be unemployed. Consequently, any recommendation for federal financial aid reform must consider this diversity and whether or not diverse institutions, like community colleges, are experiencing undue burdens because of this diversity.

Direct Subsidies.   Therefore, our first policy recommendation is to consider direct federal or state subsidies to community colleges rather than continue a costly, labor-intensive process of federal financial aid through individual students, especially at extremely "poor" institutions (Shepard, 2014). This shift can reduce the time and money colleges spend in supervising and policing the process through which students apply for, secure, and resecure their aid each semester. Reform efforts such as "Tennessee Promise" enable students to attend community colleges for free for 2 years by providing state money for tuition and fees not covered by other scholarships or grant aid programs. Although this initiative still requires completion of the FAFSA, it eliminates some of the many problematic financial aid policy hurdles that students must navigate to attend college and remain enrolled. In his 2015 State of the Union Address, President Obama announced an initiative called America's College Promise to provide two years of free community college. The idea has gained momentum in individual cities (Chicago, Philadelphia, Washington D.C.) and colleges (Harper College, Sinclair Community College), and in the states of Oregon, New York, Minnesota, and several other states proposing similar legislation. Goldrick-Rab and Kendall (2014) push the idea of such policy reforms beyond tuition coverage and make recommendations to increase the Pell grant amount to include coverage of books and supplies, plus opportunities for employment and a stipend. This overhaul would eliminate many of the challenges students and staff expressed in our research. Community college staff and administrators can begin informing state governments to move in the direction of such reforms.

Improved Information Dissemination. In the absence of such massive overhaul, our second recommendation focuses on immediate efforts to simply improve the dissemination of information to students. We emphasize social media as a particularly cost-effective tool to reach out to thousands of students instantly. In our research, we find students do respond to repetition and timely messages about general financial aid rules and processes via social media announcements. Relying on social media for generally applicable information can free time and resources for needed personalized one-on-one advising and counseling for students more directly about concrete and manageable strategies for receiving and maintaining their aid, both of which are necessities given the diversity of community college students. Although the app may have some negative consequences such as inaccurate information, as students with different experiences and contexts attempt to assist each other or angry and frustrated posts that produce a negative climate for staff, it provides an efficient way to communicate and a window into student experiences.

Better Data Collection. Given such available information, our third recommendation is for college leaders to support financial aid offices in developing data collection in a way that allows staff and leaders to make informed and better decisions to support their students, especially those in most financial need. This concretely means assessing the number and type of questions typically asked by students contacting or visiting the office, tracking the various ways information is distributed, its effectiveness, and the time it takes to respond to students. It also means using these data to test the assumptions of staff and administrators. For example, how many students enroll and then leave the institution after they receive federal financial aid? Institutions can rely on social media technology to systematically collect data on students and student experiences. Staff can learn more about areas of financial aid that students experience as problematic and possibly offer assistance through a channel that helps create transparent and time efficient dissemination of information.

More Flexible Disbursement. Our final recommendation is to consider disbursing Pell grant aid much earlier or at multiple times throughout the semester, thus reducing risk and allowing students to buy their classroom supplies and materials on-time. Colleges that choose to instead disburse aid after classes start should consider providing students with a more flexible debit option during the 30-day period that moves beyond a simple bookstore credit. A more flexible approach would allow students to better maximize their resources by buying course materials elsewhere more cost effectively and/or dealing with other expenses.

Conclusion

Federal financial aid was designed to help students, but implementation of federal policy stipulations is often experienced as punitive by the diverse population of students receiving federal financial aid. Policy regulation and the related policing of aid and climate of penalty experienced by students may be producing inequities for community college students. This raises social justice concerns in an era in which college attainment is so crucial, particularly for students in poverty struggling to achieve a credential. We believe that our recommendations will begin to relieve some of the stress and frustration students experience as they navigate processes established by perhaps well-intended policies and regulations. Perhaps raised awareness and incremental change, at both the federal level and at individual institutions, will be the first steps toward a policy system that acknowledges and encourages the strengths of students seeking financial aid to continue their education, instead of policing and punishing them by creating a climate of penalty, unnecessary hurdles, and potential inequities.

References

Advisory Committee on Student Financial Assistance. (2008). *Apply to succeed: Ensuring community college students benefit from need-based financial aid.* Washington, DC: U.S. Department of Education.

Baime, D., & Mullin, C. (2011, July). *Promoting educational opportunity: The Pell grant program at community colleges* (Policy Brief 2011-03PBL). Washington, DC: American Association of Community Colleges.

Bettinger, E. P., Long, B. T., Oreopoulos, P., & Sanbonmatsu, L. (2012). The role of application assistance and information in college decisions: Results from the H&R Block FAFSA Experiment. *The Quarterly Journal of Economics, 127*(3), 1205–1242.

College Board. (2013). *Trends in student aid, 2013.* New York, NY: The College Board Advocacy and Policy Center.

Goldrick-Rab, S., & Kendall, N. (2014, April). *F2CO. Redefining college affordability: Securing America's future with a free two-year college option.* Lumina Foundation. Retrieved from http://www.luminafoundation.org/files/publications/ideas_summit/Redefining_College_Affordability.pdf

Long, B. T. (2010). *Financial aid: A key to community college student success.* Issue Brief prepared for the White House Summit on Community Colleges.

McKinney, L., & Novak, H. (2013). The relationship between FAFSA filing and persistence among first-year community college students. *Community College Review, 41*(1), 63–85.

Mendoza, P., Mendez, J. P., & Malcolm, Z. (2009). Financial aid and persistence in community colleges: Assessing the effectiveness of federal and state financial aid programs in Oklahoma. *Community College Review, 37*(2), 112–135.

Shepard, N. (2014, June 24). Free college: State covers students' first two years. *Gb Tribune.* Retrieved from http://www.gbtribune.com/section/212/article/74304/

U.S. Department of Education. (2014, April 26). *Calculating Pell grant lifetime eligibility used.* Retrieved from http://studentaid.ed.gov/types/grants-scholarships/pell/calculate-eligibility

COURTNEY A. CAMPBELL is a doctoral student in the Department of Educational Policy Studies and Practice at the University of Arizona.

REGINA DEIL-AMEN is a professor in the Center for the Study of Higher Education/Education Policy Studies and Practice Department at the University of Arizona.

CECILIA RIOS-AGUILAR is an associate professor in the Higher Education and Organizational Change Division, Graduate School of Education and Information Studies at the University of California Los Angeles (UCLA).

NEW DIRECTIONS FOR COMMUNITY COLLEGES • DOI: 10.1002/cc

7

This chapter outlines the birth and growth of a veterans' program in Salt Lake City, Utah, and discusses next steps in spurring additional innovations and advancements to improve service for student veterans in community colleges.

Salt Lake Community College Veterans Services: A Model of Serving Veterans in Higher Education

Aaron Ahern, Michael Foster, Darlene Head

In 1944, the U.S. Congress passed legislation granting educational benefits to veterans of the Second World War. The GI Bill, as it is commonly known, would eventually allow nearly 8 million veterans to participate in higher education or postsecondary vocational training, representing nearly half of all veterans to serve in World War Two (U.S. Department of Veterans Affairs, 2015). The GI Bill provided access to postwar veterans on an unprecedented scale and continues to do so today. In 2015, after nearly 14 years of warfare, a new generation of veterans are returning home and many will face new and unique challenges that may impede their access to postsecondary education.

In 2012, more than 5% of all U.S. postsecondary students were veterans or were serving in the military, with approximately 43% attending community colleges. Over 1 million military personnel and veterans are currently attending postsecondary educational institutions, but their enrollment represents only about a third of all eligible veterans aged 18–40 (Radford, 2011; U.S. Department of Education, 2013, U.S. Department of Veterans Affairs, 2012, 2014b). It is difficult to determine exactly what barriers prevent eligible veterans from accessing postsecondary education, but many of the challenges they face are well known. For example, student veterans are likely to be older than traditional college students and are more likely to have external obligations such as being married and/or raising children (DiRamio, 2011). In many respects, student veterans are similar to other nontraditional students, but this group also experiences unique challenges that set

NEW DIRECTIONS FOR COMMUNITY COLLEGES, no. 172, Winter 2015 © 2015 Wiley Periodicals, Inc.
Published online in Wiley Online Library (wileyonlinelibrary.com) • DOI: 10.1002/cc.20165

it apart. These challenges also make it more difficult for student veterans to adequately engage with campus services and to successfully complete their education.

This chapter provides an overview of contemporary challenges faced by student veterans and highlights services provided by Salt Lake Community College, located in Salt Lake City, Utah. Salt Lake Community College (SLCC) has consistently been recognized as one of the "Best for Vets" community colleges in the country, recently ranking #11 in the *Military Times* 2014 rankings. Our chapter outlines the birth and growth of our veteran program as both an example of what can be implemented to serve our student veterans and a discussion of next steps to spur additional innovations and advancements for student veterans.

Introduction

The great majority of student veterans have been deployed to a combat zone, some with multiple deployments. More and more frequently, veterans are injured rather than killed in combat due to advancements in body armor, coagulants, and modern evacuation systems, meaning that they return to the United States with life-altering injuries. Although mortality rates are decreasing, the survivors of these conflicts are left with conditions that can be very limiting. Nearly half of the approximately 2 million veterans who served in the conflict labeled by the U.S. government as the global "War on Terror" are expected to file for disability benefits through the Veterans Administration (Church, 2009). The most common disabilities reported by student veterans are related to issues of mental health and among these, depression and posttraumatic stress disorder (PTSD) are the most frequent. However, traumatic brain injury and orthopedic concerns are also commonly reported.

Each of the aforementioned conditions can significantly hamper a veteran's educational progress. Mental health conditions such as depression and PTSD are frequently associated with poor concentration and memory as well as interpersonal difficulty and disturbance in motivation. All of these symptoms can pose obstacles to academic success. Orthopedic concerns can be associated with chronic pain and physical limitations, which can also influence concentration, motivation, and learning. Traumatic brain injuries can present with several varied symptoms; however, most are characterized by poor concentration and memory. Unfortunately, although increasing numbers of veterans file for disability through the Veterans Administration (VA) as they discharge from active duty, veterans frequently do not self-identify as experiencing disabilities and do not register for services on campus. As a result, many veterans do not receive appropriate academic accommodations and support.

Additional challenges that are unique to the student veteran population include difficulty adjusting or readjusting to school after being deployed to a combat zone and difficulty negotiating identity roles as military versus civilian. Student veterans may have difficulty relating to more traditional students and faculty and staff who do not share similar military experiences. To that end, student veterans have reported that they believe faculty do not understand what they are experiencing as student veterans because large numbers of administrators and faculty have little firsthand knowledge of the military and military culture. Finally, veterans report experiencing difficulty in successfully navigating their educational benefits through the GI Bill.

The challenges facing colleges and universities in serving student veterans are significant and several suggestions have been found in the literature to improve services available to student veterans and military personnel. Among these suggestions are the following:

- Colleges and universities should aid veterans in integrating into student veteran peer groups and/or meeting with peer mentors (Church, 2009; DiRamio, 2011).
- Campus providers should be trained in providing empirically based treatments for PTSD (Rudd, Goulding, & Bryan, 2011).
- Veterans should be aided by college staff in developing civilian equivalents of skills and qualities developed in the military (DiRamio, 2011).
- Campuses need to be prepared to provide mental health services and support to veterans (Ackerman, DiRamio, & Garza Mitchell, 2009).
- Campuses need to increase sensitivity and understanding of the needs of veterans when creating policy (Ackerman et al., 2009).
- A creative and flexible approach should be taken to increase use of disability resource centers on campus by student veterans (Shackelford, 2009).
- Campuses should partner with veteran service organizations, with specific emphasis placed on partnering with VA vocational rehabilitation, vet centers (which are outpatient facilities that provide readjustment counseling to combat veterans and their families), and VA medical centers (Burnett & Segoria, 2009; Rumann & Hamrick, 2009).
- It is important to integrate services so that VA staff members can be located on college campuses to facilitate access to critical services, including health care and mental health treatment (Smith-Osborne, 2012).
- It is important that administrators, faculty, and staff receive education to increase knowledge and skill in working with veterans and military personnel (Burnett & Segoria, 2009; DiRamio, Ackerman, & Mitchell, 2008; Moon & Schma, 2011; Rumann & Hamrick, 2009; U.S. Department of Veterans Affairs, 2014a).

Addressing Challenges to the Student Veteran Community and Increasing Accessibility

Salt Lake Community College is committed to meeting the needs of the veteran population through partnerships with various community programs as well as dedicated college resources to assist veterans pursuing their educational goals. In recognition of the unique challenges that veterans face in obtaining their education, the college created a new department within student services, called Veterans Services, and provided an operating budget that would enable services and support for veterans to be coordinated under this department. Since the creation of the Veterans Services department, staff have been developing collaborative relationships that increase accessibility and streamline sometimes cumbersome systems.

Development of Salt Lake Community College Veterans Center

With an influx of new student veterans arriving on campus, the veteran population grew from 663 in the Fall 2006 semester to 832 in the Fall 2009 semester. The Salt Lake Community College administration recognized the varied and increased needs of this population and the need to have a space large enough to provide the multiple services that both the school and community organizations could offer. Prior to 2007, services for veterans were provided in a 178-square-foot room located in the SLCC student center. Given the increased number of veterans and the increasingly complex set of services the school would need to provide, it was obvious that this space was insufficient. The proposal to establish a veterans' center at SLCC was developed in 2007. The goal was to provide a "one-stop shop" where veterans could receive information about all aspects of their college experience and access services unique to their circumstances. This includes college resources such as admissions, registration, and disability resources, as well as VA services such as education benefits, disability information, health care information and enrollment, employment information, tutoring services, and accommodation needs. By providing these services in one central location, veterans can have many of their needs met without having to navigate these complex systems by themselves.

In 2008, SLCC dedicated space for a new veterans' center with an area of over 1500 square feet. The facility includes offices for SLCC employees to process veterans' education benefits as well as offices for VA personnel and other community partners. The center also features a lounge for veterans with couches, chairs, a television, and other amenities provided by the SLCC administration. Additionally, space was allocated within the center to serve as a computer lab containing several computers. The center's staff had noticed that veterans with PTSD, many of whom experience a tendency to be constantly being on guard and watchful, found working in a student computer lab with hundreds of other students in a large room emotionally distressing and caused distraction. The computer lab in the SLCC Veterans Center was created to provide a smaller space and a greater sense of security for veterans, allowing them to concentrate on their work rather than being distracted by the student traffic that is typical for a college computer lab.

NEW DIRECTIONS FOR COMMUNITY COLLEGES • DOI: 10.1002/cc

Social Support.   Interaction with fellow veterans can facilitate a student veteran's transition into campus life. The center's lounge area was developed to provide veterans with a safe space in which to decompress and relax from the stress of school and to interact with other veterans who have shared many similar experiences. SLCC Veterans Services also participates in the VA workstudy employment program, often employing 10 student veterans in the center. This program provides an opportunity to employ veterans who can help with processing paperwork and benefits for other veterans on campus. Additionally, these veterans can act as informal mentors to new veterans on campus, often being the first contact on campus for these new students.

The Veterans Services staff have also sponsored and supported a local chapter of the Student Veterans of America, providing veterans with the opportunity to meet with each other on a regular basis and taking action to serve other veterans and the community. In addition, some student veterans at SLCC have had the opportunity to meet with a peer mentor to discuss their needs and to be made aware of benefits and services available to them. Peer mentors are fellow student veterans with experience at Salt Lake Community College who have received training provided at the VA medical center regarding working with other veterans and accessing educational benefits. Meeting with peer mentors is a long-standing tradition in military services academies and is supported by contemporary literature as beneficial. As such, the peer mentoring program has recently been expanded and a peer mentor is now available to all new student veterans as part of their orientation to campus. The peer mentor then maintains an ongoing relationship with the student veteran, providing guidance and support throughout the student's academic career.

Disability Resource Services.   Historically, veterans had been reluctant to use the college's Disability Resource Center (DRC). Underuse of services is perhaps not surprising given contemporary literature and research. Some student veterans avoid identifying themselves with a disability because doing so could be perceived as a weakness. To help remove the possible stigma of disability and potential difficulty resulting from admission of perceived weakness, Veterans Services and the DRC creatively collaborated to address this issue. A DRC advisor keeps regular office hours in the Veterans Center, and the position title has been changed to veterans accessibility advisor. By removing the term "disability" from the position description and being available to meet with veterans in the Veterans Center, the social stigma that may have prevented veterans from accessing academic accommodations may have decreased. For example, in the 2013–2014 academic year, the DRC nearly doubled the numbers of veterans served. We believe that this increase is due in large part to the title change of the counselor. Additionally, the veterans accessibility advisor, who is housed in the Veterans Center, has been instrumental in our efforts to serve student veterans. The accessibility advisor works to accommodate the needs of veterans with

NEW DIRECTIONS FOR COMMUNITY COLLEGES • DOI: 10.1002/cc

PTSD and traumatic brain injury, the signature injuries of the current conflicts, through provision of note takers, extended testing times, and other accommodations that may assist them in relationship to their disabilities. By having a veterans accessibility advisor in the Veterans Center, services can be provided while minimizing the potential stigma of disability.

Partnership with the Department of Veterans Affairs. The relationship between SLCC and the VA has also been a key component to meeting veterans needs on campus. In 2009, the VA established VetSuccess On Campus (VSOC) as a pilot program on eight campuses throughout the country to assist veterans returning to the classroom. Through application to the Veterans Benefits Administration of the VA, SLCC was selected as one of these campuses. This program provides a full-time VA vocational rehabilitation counselor to be housed at SLCC in the Veterans Center and funded by the Department of Veterans Affairs. Currently there are more than 75 campuses throughout the country with VetSuccess on Campus counselors working full time on college campuses to assist veterans transitioning from the military to an academic environment. The VSOC counselor at SLCC provides transitional assistance from military service to school. As noted previously, this transition can be difficult due to cultural differences between academia and the military. The VSOC counselor works to facilitate this transition. This counselor also provides educational and occupational counseling and guidance to veterans on campus and can help them map out their educational and career goals while using their prior military experience and training as well as their VA educational benefits. The VSOC counselor also provides information and facilitates access to VA benefits. This service aids veterans in applying for various VA benefits without having to navigate the complex VA benefits system alone, allowing veterans to focus on their educational pursuits.

In order to increase accessibility to VA health care, in 2012 a partnership between SLCC and another VA initiative, Veterans Integration to Academic Leadership (VITAL), was developed. The VITAL program coordinator is in the Veterans Center at SLCC 2 days a week and represents the local VA medical center. The VITAL coordinator engages in outreach to make veterans aware of the health care services available to them and helps them navigate the VA health care system from enrolling them for services to helping them to connect with appropriate providers. The VITAL coordinator is also a mental health professional and provides mental health services on campus, including empirically based treatments for posttraumatic stress disorder, as well as testing for learning disabilities and attention-deficit/hyperactivity disorder. In addition, the VITAL coordinator develops collaborative relationships with campus and community organizations and provides information to the campus community regarding working with student veterans. This often takes the form of on-campus training for faculty and staff. These trainings are often presented in partnership between the VITAL coordinator, the VetSuccess on Campus counselor, and the veterans services manager, with each presenting information pertinent to his or her area of specialization.

Community Collaboration.   In addition to partnering with the Department of Veterans Affairs, SLCC has also developed partnerships with various state agencies and programs to assist veterans. One example of this partnership is with the Utah Department of Workforce Services (DWS), which provides a disabled veteran outreach placement specialist (DVOP) on campus weekly. This individual provides employment assistance to veterans who may have employment needs not met through the school's Employment Center. Many employers may have veteran hiring programs and recruit specifically through DWS, and as such, the SLCC Employment Center may not have access to employment opportunities for these student veterans. Additionally, the DVOP can work with veterans individually to assist them in translating their military experience and training into more civilian friendly language. DWS also has funding available to assist veterans in their training goals through the Workforce Investment Act. Having a DVOP on campus on a weekly basis provides this information and access to veterans who may be seeking these funds to achieve their educational and occupational goals and provides other state emergency funds when needed such as food stamps, Medicaid support, and utility emergency funds.

Veterans Services has also developed and maintained numerous other community partnerships and aligned with already institutionalized programming in order to strengthen viability and streamline services. Examples of these partners include Veterans Upward Bound- TRIO Program, the National Veteran Program Administrators (NAVPA), the OIF/OEF (Operation Iraqi Freedom and Operation Enduring Freedom) Advisory Team, AmeriCorps, Salt Lake County Veterans Small Business Development Subcommittee, the Utah Veterans and Military Employment Coalition, Utah Wasatch Front Army Recruiting Battalion Advisory Board, Utah Veterans Education and Training Working Group, Helmets to Hardhats, the Utah Yellow Ribbon Support Team, the Utah National Guard Education Fair Committee, and the Utah Veterans Job Fairs Committee. Through these community partnerships, student veterans at SLCC are able to have access to information about these various programs in one setting. These services help veterans with employment transition assistance, funding for training, and other community services. Additionally, these community service providers are able to have easier access to their target demographic audience.

Recommendations

Every college is unique and programs listed in this chapter may or may not be available in every area, but it is our hope that some of the SLCC experience can generalize to other schools in similar circumstances. Administratively the creation of a department dedicated to veterans has been

NEW DIRECTIONS FOR COMMUNITY COLLEGES • DOI: 10.1002/cc

very helpful. Individuals who desire to create such a department should work with appropriate college leadership to help them to recognize and support such an effort. Additionally, commitment of space dedicated to student veterans is significant and provides the possibility of broader collaboration with government and community agencies. Because each college and area of the country will have different organizations and resources available, it is difficult to give more than superficial recommendations in this area; however, one organization that will be available in most areas is the Department of Veterans Affairs. College administrators should reach out to the VA organizations in their area to discuss ways in which the VA can provide support to on-campus efforts. Similarly, college administrators should perform outreach to community organizations dedicated to serving veterans and develop appropriate partnerships.

Conclusion

There is much more to be done to serve student veterans in community colleges if we are to help this current crop of veterans to become the next "greatest generation" with all of the positive societal impacts resulting from the first "greatest generation."

By developing a veteran services department and providing a center that allows student veterans to receive services in a "one-stop" area, SLCC has been able to demonstrate its commitment to veteran success educationally and in the workforce. In addition to national recognition for the services being provided to veterans on campus, veteran enrollment has increased and the numbers of veterans graduating continues to increase. Since 2008, SLCC has seen a steady growth in the numbers of student veterans using their VA educational benefits to enroll in degree and certificate programs: from 522 veterans enrolled in 2008 to 1283 enrolled in 2013. Although the numbers of veterans enrolling at SLCC continues to increase, the most encouraging result is the numbers of veterans completing training programs. In 2008, 34 individuals using VA education programs graduated or completed their certification programs. In 2014, that number increased to 201.

These numbers, although encouraging, do not suggest causality and efforts are being made to develop systematic research that can adequately measure the impact of the center and its interventions. Although there is certainly more work to be done in helping veterans to overcome challenges facing them in higher education and efforts need to be placed on systematically tracking the efficacy of our current interventions, the center's design and services are consistent with recommendations from current literature. Current literature suggests that integrating VA and campus resources, training faculty and staff, and applying flexible measures to increase accessibility to disability resource center services are at the forefront of innovations in facing these challenges. SLCC Veterans Services is committed to evolve and will continue to provide a model of best practices moving forward. By removing many of the barriers to success for veterans on campus, they can play an active role in the community on campus, and more importantly, move on to a successful life using the benefits they have earned through their sacrifice and hard work.

References

Ackerman, R., DiRamio, D., & Garza Mitchell, R. L. (2009). Transitions: Combat veterans as college students. In R. Ackerman & D. DiRamio (Eds.), *New Directions for Student Services: No. 126. Creating a veteran-friendly campus: Strategies for transition success* (pp. 5–14). San Francisco, CA: Jossey-Bass.

Burnett, S. E., & Segoria, J. (2009). Collaboration on military transition students from combat to college: It takes a community. *Journal of Postsecondary Education and Disability, 22*(1), 53–58.

Church, T. E. (2009). Returning veterans on campus with war-related injuries and the long road back home. *Journal of Postsecondary Education and Disability, 22*(1), 43–52.

DiRamio, D. (2011). *Transition 2.0: Using Tinto's model to understand student-veteran persistence* (ASHE Higher Education Report, Vol. 37, No. 3). San Francisco, CA: Jossey-Bass.

DiRamio, D., Ackerman, R., & Mitchell, R. L. (2008). From combat to campus: Voices of student-veterans. *NASPA Journal, 45*(1), 73–102.

Military Times. (2014). *Best for vets: Colleges 2014, 2-year schools.* Retrieved from http://projects.militarytimes.com/jobs/best-for-vets/2014/colleges/2-year/

Moon, T. L., & Schma, G. A. (2011). A proactive approach to serving military and veteran students. In J. B. Hodson & B. W. Speck (Eds.), *New Directions for Higher Education: No. 153. Entrepreneurship in student services* (pp. 53–60). San Francisco, CA: Jossey-Bass.

Radford, A. W. (2011). *Military service members and veterans: A profile of those enrolled in undergraduate and graduate education in 2007–08* (Stats in Brief, NCES 2011-163). Washington, DC: National Center for Education Statistics, U.S. Department of Education.

Rudd, M. D., Goulding, J., & Bryan, C. J. (2011). Student veterans: A national survey exploring psychological symptoms and suicide risk. *Professional Psychology: Research and Practice, 42*(5), 354–360. doi:10.1037/a0025164

Rumann, C. B., & Hamrick, F. A. (2009). Supporting student veterans in transition. In R. Ackerman & D. DiRamio (Eds.), *New Directions for Student Services: No. 126. Creating a veteran-friendly campus: Strategies for transition success* (pp. 25–34). San Francisco, CA: Jossey-Bass.

Shackelford, A. L. (2009). Documenting the needs of student veterans with disabilities: Intersection roadblocks, solutions, and legal realities. *Journal of Postsecondary Education and Disability, 22*(1), 36–42.

Smith-Osborne, A. (2012). Supported education for returning veterans with PTSD and other mental disorders. *Journal of Rehabilitation, 78*(2), 4–12.

U.S. Department of Education. (2013). Table 303.25. Total fall enrollment in degree-granting postsecondary institutions, by control and level of institution: 1970 through 2012. *Digest of Education Statistics.* Retrieved from http://nces.ed.gov/programs/digest/d13/tables/dt13_303.25.asp

U.S. Department of Veterans Affairs. (2012). *Veterans Benefits Administration annual report.* Retrieved from http://www.vba.va.gov/REPORTS/

U.S. Department of Veterans Affairs. (2014a). *FY 2014–2020 strategic plan.* Retrieved from http://www.va.gov/performance/

U.S. Department of Veterans Affairs. (2014b). *VetPop 2014: Living veterans by age group, gender*. Retrieved from http://www.va.gov/vetdata/veteran_population.asp
U.S. Department of Veterans Affairs. (2015). *History and timeline*. Retrieved from http://www.benefits.va.gov/gibill/history.asp

AARON AHERN, PHD, *is program coordinator for VITAL at the Department of Veterans Affairs Medical Center in Salt Lake City.*

MICHAEL FOSTER, PHD, *works for the Department of Veterans Affairs as the Vet-Success on campus counselor at Salt Lake Community College.*

DARLENE HEAD *is director of Veterans Services at Salt Lake Community College.*

NEW DIRECTIONS FOR COMMUNITY COLLEGES • DOI: 10.1002/cc

8

This chapter introduces Institutional Undocu-Competence (IUC), an institutional capacity framework emerging from a critical analysis of cultural competence, aimed to inform community colleges' efforts to better support the growing undocumented student population.

Undocumented Students at the Community College: Creating Institutional Capacity

*Jéssica I. Valenzuela, William Perez, Iliana Perez,
Gloria Itzel Montiel, Gabriel Chaparro*

As undocumented students become more represented on college campuses, there is a growing need to establish appropriate institutional practices to support them. Community colleges serve as the primary gateway to higher education for undocumented students due to the significant savings in tuition costs and the flexibility in enrollment options, yet few studies have examined how institutions can build capacity to support undocumented student enrollment, retention, and academic success (e.g., Chen, 2013). The unfair treatment of undocumented immigrants in their pursuit of higher education is well documented in prior research and thus will not be addressed in depth in this chapter (e.g., Pérez, 2010, 2011). Rather, the present chapter proposes clear steps toward strengthening what we call Institutional Undocu-Competence (IUC), an institutional capacity framework, to assess how well community colleges are serving this student population.

IUC emerges from a critique of cultural competence (Kumagai & Lypson, 2009). Cultural competence in higher education has largely focused on merely promoting awareness of diversity and equality while failing to hold institutions accountable for changes to improve equity for underserved populations with particular needs, such as undocumented students. IUC draws from social justice frameworks by demanding action from institutions serving undocumented students. Our previous research suggests that in order for institutions of higher education to build IUC they must

NEW DIRECTIONS FOR COMMUNITY COLLEGES, no. 172, Winter 2015 © 2015 Wiley Periodicals, Inc.
Published online in Wiley Online Library (wileyonlinelibrary.com) • DOI: 10.1002/cc.20166

challenge themselves by training faculty and staff, advocating for students, building appropriate college outreach and recruitment procedures, increasing financial aid, supporting undocumented student organizations on campus, providing appropriate health and psychological services, and creating a visible welcoming campus environment. The following section provides a discussion of the necessary steps to develop IUC.

Why Are Undocumented Students an Equity Issue?

The U.S. higher education system has made important progress in the past decade to increase the enrollment, retention, and degree completion of immigrant students. However, undocumented students continue to face campus marginalization and discrimination. To be fully inclusive of all immigrant students, higher education institutions need to focus on addressing the various challenges faced by undocumented students (Dozier, 1995).

The lack of federal immigration reform laws has resulted in a wide range of localized enforcement of immigration laws that vary dramatically from state to state. Whereas some states have adopted policies that extend the rights of immigrant communities including eligibility for drivers' licenses, student loans, and professional licenses, other states have adopted policies that are restrictive and punitive in nature, denying basic needs such as health care and education and criminalizing undocumented status. In light of the variability of contexts that undocumented students navigate, we call on institutions of higher education to consistently and openly support this underserved population.

Policy and Assessment Recommendations

Given the risks associated with disclosing immigration status and the potential fear of retribution faced by students and their advocates and allies, campus policies should ensure confidentiality. Furthermore, institutions should make their position in support of undocumented students clear and visible through written policy so as to prevent stigmatization of undocumented students by deeming their presence a secret. Such policies would encourage students to seek necessary academic and social support and participate in campus assessment efforts without fear of disclosing their status.

IUC embraces an understanding of the resilience to the challenges faced by undocumented students. In order to better understand undocumented student needs, institutions must implement a campus assessment centered on the input of undocumented students while considering the experiences of advocates and allies. Various data collection methods should be implemented in order to obtain diverse input. For example, focus groups and one-on-one interviews may provide depth and breadth of data from students who feel comfortable sharing their experience with school staff, faculty, and administration. Anonymous online survey methods may complement this information with input from students who either do not feel comfortable sharing their experiences openly or whose time demands do not allow for them to meet with school representatives beyond their academic responsibilities.

Institutional assessments should examine and modify administrative procedures that may inadvertently stigmatize students. For example, many undocumented students have been discouraged from applying to college or completing their degrees due to their status by recruitment or financial aid staff who are not properly trained to answer undocumented students' questions about the support available to them. Another example is when students find out an application for admissions does not allow for them to select "Consideration of Deferred Action for Childhood Arrivals (DACA) recipient" or "undocumented" as their legal status and they are forced to choose an option that does not accurately describe their experience and needs. Yet another example is when undocumented students are wrongfully classified as international students. These examples are a few of many processes that stigmatize students by not recognizing their unique circumstances in institutional policies or procedures to validate their presence within the student body.

Because immigration policies change constantly, IUC needs assessment should be a continuous and ongoing process. Although institutional assessment results may vary depending on local contexts, in the next section we provide several suggestions based on previous research as a starting point for institutions to gather baseline information. Undocumented students' needs include specifically tailored college outreach and recruitment, advocacy, financial aid, institutional support for student groups, and mental health services. IUC requires action on behalf of the institution and its representatives, placing training of college faculty and staff at the core of its execution. The importance of training college faculty and staff is discussed in the next section followed by an in-depth discussion of students' needs.

Training College Faculty and Staff

Training college faculty and staff is one of the first steps toward IUC because it solidifies the institution's commitment to undocumented students. School personnel need to be knowledgeable about the unique circumstances that limit undocumented student enrollment, retention, transfer, and graduation. Once faculty, counselors, admissions staff, financial aid officers, and registrars are informed, they will be better able to establish institutional policies and procedures to reduce instances of exclusion and marginality. The risks and stigma associated with disclosing their undocumented status make finding allies an arduous process for undocumented students. Students may erroneously assume that professionals or faculty who share their ethnic background will be sympathetic to their situation only to find the opposite to be true upon disclosing their status. Undocumented students are often scrutinized and humiliated by admissions and registrar office personnel when they seek services and as a consequence, they develop great anxiety. Furthermore, undocumented students often experience microaggressions in the form of intentional and unintentional everyday insults, indignities, and demeaning messages that perpetuate inequities by conveying oppressive ideologies. IUC training should include ways to identify and address microaggressions directed at undocumented students.

The more informed student affairs professionals are about the sociopolitical contexts of undocumented students' lives, the better they can meet their needs. IUC training should include information about the local, state, and federal laws that affect undocumented students at that particular institution. It is of utmost importance that IUC training highlights the value of undocumented students' contributions, their resilience, and their legal rights. When undocumented students see that student affairs professionals know about and demonstrate an ethic of care, it increases the likelihood of developing trust, which can result in higher use of student support services and further assist student affairs professionals in supporting students' academic achievement and personal growth.

Visible and Open Advocacy

Colleges should establish visible networks of allies to facilitate information dissemination across the campus community. One of the best ways community college personnel can serve undocumented students is to become visible advocates for them. IUC calls for advocates and allies to make themselves visible to undocumented students because their risk of disclosure as advocate/ally is relatively lower than the risk of disclosure faced by a student as an undocumented immigrant. Self-identification as advocates and allies by campus personnel reaffirms the institution's commitment to serving undocumented students (Pérez, Munoz, Alcantar, & Guarneros, 2011).

Advocacy is central to student affairs work, and it should not be restricted to students' lives on campus. Rather, advocacy should include recognition of the ways that the legal and policy contexts off campus shape community college students' lives. Community college administrators can also work to build coalitions and partnerships with grassroots and community-based organizations (CBOs) that advocate for immigrants' rights. Principles of social justice counseling can also guide efforts to support undocumented students. These efforts should involve addressing issues such as poverty, pollution, health care access, street violence, and institutional racism through psychoeducational workshops and conferences in order to promote awareness and further encourage advocacy.

Community college advocates and allies should build trust with undocumented students by demonstrating an ethic of care, justice, and autonomy. Students share sensitive information with individuals whom they feel they can trust and who can provide honest, direct, and informed advice while protecting their confidentiality. Therefore, it is important for faculty and staff to create safe environments for students by demonstrating an awareness of the challenges that undocumented students face. It is critical to be sensitive when a student chooses to disclose his or her immigration status and even more critical for school personnel to disclose themselves as advocates and allies. The training of school personnel that IUC calls for is a building block for establishing the trust necessary to identify students' needs, and advocate for students.

College Outreach and Recruitment

College outreach and recruitment are other important areas that require new solutions to the admissions and matriculation difficulties faced by undocumented students. Effective college outreach and recruitment efforts need to consider the ways in which undocumented students are systematically excluded from participation in college-prep activities in high school. With a deeper understanding of undocumented students, community colleges can create more effective collaborations with high schools and baccalaureate-awarding institutions to substantially increase undocumented students' pathways to higher education (Pérez, 2010).

IUC sets the discussion of institutional support for undocumented students within specific local contexts and calls for active collaboration among institutions. A recommendation for establishing these collaborations would be to identify an IUC committee of staff, faculty, and students at each institution to meet on a regular basis with the IUC committees of nearby institutions to share their progress on strengthening IUC and ways participating institutions can support each other. The meetings of IUC committees should take place among and between high schools, community colleges, baccalaureate-awarding institutions, and graduate professional schools.

It is important to disseminate information about the matriculation process for undocumented students, scholarship and student services programs, and transfer information to high school educators and students. IUC requires that student affairs professionals expand their outreach and recruitment beyond the traditional mechanisms of college fairs, campus visits, and high school visits. Because undocumented students may be afraid to seek out information, it is imperative that they are provided with information on opportunities for legal employment, higher education opportunities, and funding for college. Outreach to undocumented students should also encompass a consistent and long-standing presence in the community to include schools and culturally relevant community locations. When undocumented students receive timely and accurate information about their postsecondary options, they are much more likely to prepare for and apply to college and complete their degrees. It is important to note that like all community college students, undocumented students enroll in community college for various reasons (Jauregui, Slate, & Stallone Brown, 2008). IUC urges the institution to identify the goals of undocumented students upon enrolling to tailor student support services accordingly.

It is important to consider that many undocumented students are also first-generation college students. In general, first-generation students select institutions based on the availability of financial aid, proximity to home, and their ability to work while enrolled. Many first-generation undocumented college students feel conflicted between their own desires to pursue postsecondary education and their sense of duty to be an integral part of their family structures. Given these and other dynamics, student affairs practitioners must consider these overlapping factors to ensure that undocumented students succeed.

Financial Aid

The financial difficulties that undocumented students encounter are among the most difficult obstacle to overcome (Chavez, Soriano, & Oliverez, 2007). Due to the cumbersome nature of the college and scholarship application processes, undocumented students require significant individualized support. The support and information they receive at school plays a large role in determining whether or not they successfully apply to college and secure financial assistance. Even in states with in-state tuition policies that make college more affordable for undocumented students, many are still unable to afford higher education.

IUC is demonstrated when community college personnel are proactive in providing all available resources for undocumented students. Waiting for students to inquire about financial aid options places the largest amount of responsibility on the student. Recognizing the microaggressions and stigmatizing experiences that undocumented students face when seeking resources from financial aid offices, IUC calls for targeted dissemination of resources. One example is creating pamphlets with financial aid information specifically for undocumented students and distributing these in resource centers, cafeterias, classrooms, and bulletin boards outside of the financial aid offices.

IUC is also demonstrated when schools reach beyond their usual limits to raise funds and advocate for undocumented students outside of the institution. Schools should work together with local philanthropic organizations and businesses to develop scholarships specifically for undocumented students. Because scholarship providers are often unaware of the challenges to college access that undocumented students encounter, the role of campus-based advocates is crucial in educating scholarship providers about the importance of extending aid to undocumented students.

Furthermore, IUC calls for institutions to explore other nontraditional ways to provide financial assistance to students such as stipends for special projects or service and awards for books and materials. Because of the vulnerable financial state of undocumented immigrant households, community colleges should provide specialized informational sessions on the pitfalls of the student loans for which undocumented students are eligible, which often involve predatory lending practices from private financial institutions and banks. IUC is defined by the institution's ability to provide necessary information and resources regarding financial aid to undocumented students and advocating on their behalf when working with philanthropic organizations.

Institutional Support for Student Groups

Undocumented-student organizations are critically important sources of support for community college students. The general lack of information among school officials about undocumented students prompted the development of student-led campus groups that provide information about higher education access to students, parents, teachers and counselors. In California, student information sharing and advocacy within higher education settings are moving an increasing number of students through California's public college and university system by drawing on the resources in their student networks. These organizations have pioneered student-initiated recruitment and retention strategies that take into account the pre-college contexts of undocumented students. They draw on the wealth of assets that current and previous undocumented students share from their actual experiences as well as academic research, institutional resources, and the participation of other student and educator allies. By centering on the social contexts of undocumented students' precollege lives, college student groups validate students' struggles to persist in higher education as undocumented students.

Continuing to recognize and support the efforts of student-led initiatives demonstrates a high level of commitment on behalf of the school, strengthening relationships between the school and students, which in turn facilitates transmission of information and quality of assessments. Recognizing student groups as official school clubs or organizations legitimizes their cause and makes funding opportunities available to support their efforts, demonstrating an ethic of autonomy and justice. Including these student groups in orientation materials and presentations demonstrates to incoming students an ethic of care.

Health and Psychological Services

Undocumented students may suffer from anxiety and fear and, as a consequence, are likely to develop mental and physical health problems that may place them at risk of dropping out if an effective support system is not in place. To strengthen IUC, the responsibility of training staff and faculty must be shifted away from the student and toward the institution in order to build trusting relationships, through which information can be transmitted. In the case of relationships with general and mental health providers, this shift is extremely important, as it is one of the most vulnerable interactions that students must navigate in college.

It is essential that school health providers, including psychologists and counselors, receive thorough training on the socioemotional experiences of undocumented students (Pérez, Cortés, Ramos, & Coronado, 2010). Workshops focusing on anxiety, alienation, depression, stress management, and posttraumatic stress disorder are just some of the services that can be tailored to undocumented students. Colleges should also facilitate student-led peer counseling and social support efforts and provide general information regarding access to health care for undocumented students. These efforts can help reduce student distress, anxiety, and other health concerns, thus reducing or eliminating a major barrier that prevents these students from applying to and persisting at the community college.

Creating a Welcoming Campus Environment

Students who can access campus resources have more opportunities to develop personal and professional skills. Undocumented students need institutional supportive staff who are sensitive and empathetic to promote engagement and foster validation. IUC calls for visible support of undocumented students and their allies at all levels of interaction with the school. One way to ensure that resources are accessible to all and that the institution's support of undocumented students is visible is to establish an office of equal standing with other student resource offices where campus-specific resources are accessible to staff, faculty, students, and potential applicants.

Institutions should also help students transfer into accredited bachelor's degree–granting institutions and plan for life after college. The identification of role models and mentors is an important component in the career development process of undocumented students. In some fields or industries, finding these mentors is a challenge, especially with the compounded element of immigration status. Career center staff should work diligently to include allies for undocumented students in their professional networks so that they can refer students to professionals who are willing to help them navigate barriers and become career mentors. Some campus career centers ensure that career counselors are well versed in the needs of undocumented students in order to customize services. These efforts facilitate their full integration into campus life and reaffirm goals beyond community college.

Conclusion

Previous research on 4-year colleges provides a good starting point for conceptualizing institutional capacity to serve undocumented students. Community colleges present a conflicting context due to substantially higher enrollment of undocumented students and disparities in the availability of institutional resources. Our research suggests that although some community colleges have implemented various efforts to recruit, enroll, and support undocumented students, others have taken few efforts, if any (Pérez, 2011; Pérez & Cortés, 2011), to support this vastly underserved population. The IUC framework asserts that it is possible to build institutional support for undocumented students through an ethic of care, justice, and autonomy.

In order to exercise IUC, community colleges should demonstrate an understanding of the challenges that undocumented students overcome in order to access and persist in higher education. Institutions should carefully balance proactively reaching out to meet undocumented students' needs while recognizing and respecting their autonomy. To do so, institutions must strengthen and tailor existing resources such as mental and physical health, career advising, and financial aid services to serve undocumented students' needs. Institutions can genuinely reach out to undocumented students by reducing the perceived social stigma of their status on campus. To do so, institutions should highlight existing networks of allies and advocates by publicly affirming their presence through institutionalized training for all personnel and by creating IUC networks across institutions. Furthermore, institutions must recognize undocumented students' resilience by openly supporting platforms through which students can exercise self-advocacy.

References

Chavez, M. L., Soriano, M., & Oliverez, P. (2007). Undocumented students' access to college: The American dream denied. *Latino Studies, 5,* 254–263.

Chen, A. C. R. (2013). *Undocumented students, institutional allies, and transformative resistance: An institutional case study.* Unpublished doctoral dissertation, University of California, Los Angeles.

Dozier, S. B. (1995). Undocumented immigrant students at an urban community college: A demographic and academic profile. *Migration World, 23*(1/2), 20–22.

Jauregui, J. A., Slate, J. R., & Stallone Brown, M. (2008). Texas community colleges and characteristics of a growing undocumented student population. *Journal of Hispanic Higher Education, 7*(4), 346–355.

Kumagai, A. K., & Lypson, M. L. (2009). Beyond cultural competence: Critical consciousness, social justice, and multicultural education. *Academic Medicine, 84*(6), 782–787.

Pérez, W. (2010). Higher education access for undocumented students: Recommendations for counseling professionals. *Journal of College Admission, 206,* 32–35.

Pérez, W. (2011). *Americans by heart: Undocumented Latino students and the promise of higher education.* New York: Teachers College Press.

Pérez, W., & Cortés, R. (2011). *Undocumented Latino college students: Their socioemotional and academic experiences.* Dallas, TX: LFB Scholarly Publishing.

Pérez, W., Cortés, R., Ramos, K., & Coronado, H. (2010). "Cursed and blessed": Examining the socioemotional and academic experiences of undocumented Latino/a college students. *New Directions for Student Services: No. 131. Understanding and supporting undocumented students* (pp. 35–51). San Francisco, CA: Jossey-Bass.

Pérez, W., Munoz, S., Alcantar, C., & Guarneros, N. (2011). Educators supporting DREAMERS: Becoming an undocumented student ally. In J. Landsman & C. W. Lewis (Eds), *White teachers/diverse classrooms: A guide to building inclusive schools, promoting high expectations, and eliminating racism* (2nd ed.). Sterling, VA: Stylus Publishing.

JÉSSICA I. VALENZUELA *is a doctoral student in the School of Educational Studies at Claremont Graduate University.*

WILLIAM PEREZ *is an associate professor in the School of Educational Studies at Claremont Graduate University.*

ILIANA PEREZ *is a doctoral student in the School of Educational Studies at Claremont Graduate University.*

GLORIA ITZEL MONTIEL *is a doctoral student in the School of Educational Studies at Claremont Graduate University. She also serves as the Grants and Contracts Coordinator at Latino Health Access.*

GABRIEL CHAPARRO *is a doctoral student in the School of Educational Studies at Claremont Graduate University.*

9

Through an illustrative example of Together We Achieve at Parkland College in Champaign, Illinois, this chapter outlines an institutional approach for improving conditions for Black men on campus.

Black Men Attending Community Colleges: Examining an Institutional Approach Toward Equity

Lorenzo Baber, Randy Fletcher, Edmund Graham

Persistent opportunity gaps for underrepresented men of Color[1] in the United States remain a significant social justice issue in our society, a core element of the community unrest and resistance observed throughout the nation over the last year. Among the targeted areas for improvement from community leaders and governmental policy makers is the strengthening of college readiness and completion among this underserved population. Research has documented the persistent disparate outcomes for underrepresented men of Color (MOC) in postsecondary education, particularly Black[2] men. In every measure related to postsecondary success—enrollment, persistence, and degree attainment—stratified outcomes for Black men's experience are observed. Among the young adult population (18–24 years old), Black men have the lowest postsecondary enrollment rates, 34%, compared to 41% overall (National Center for Education Statistics, 2014). Black men have the highest percentage of postsecondary attrition at both 2-year (79%) and 4-year (65%) institutions (National Center for Education Statistics, 2012). Whereas 30% of the working adult population (25–64 years old) holds a postsecondary credential, the proportion is 18% among Black working adult men.

A growing body of research on underrepresented men of Color in postsecondary education focuses on those attending 2-year institutions. Community colleges serve as a primary postsecondary pathway for underrepresented men of Color. Wood, Palmer, and Harris (2015) report that nearly 72% of Black men in postsecondary education begin at a community

NEW DIRECTIONS FOR COMMUNITY COLLEGES, no. 172, Winter 2015 © 2015 Wiley Periodicals, Inc.
Published online in Wiley Online Library (wileyonlinelibrary.com) • DOI: 10.1002/cc.20167

college, making the 2-year context an important site for educational equity. Similar to general scholarship on men of Color in higher education, however, research on those attending community colleges tends to emphasize psychological paradigms to address disparate outcomes. Although individual resistance to structural norms (e.g., "grit") is a component of success, it cannot fully explain disparate outcomes within social institutions. This approach limits attention to constitutive influences of structural practices that contribute to shaping individual actions within a social system. Kezar (2011) amplifies the importance of focusing on institutional policies and practices when addressing inequalities in higher education. An individual focus on reducing disparate outcomes for underrepresented men of Color is problematic as it supports meritocratic ideology in higher education and cultural deficit perspectives. As Castro (Chapter 1) describes, persistence of outcome inequalities in community college contexts requires new approaches to better address the roots of disparate opportunity.

The purpose of this chapter is to enable community college leaders to identify institutional barriers and consider organizational changes that support success among underrepresented men of Color. First, we briefly summarize current social realities and institutional practices that disproportionately shape outcomes for underrepresented men of Color attending community colleges. Next, we present an illustrative example of an institutional approach in addressing inequalities for Black men—the Together We Achieve (TWA) program at Parkland College in Champaign, Illinois. We conclude the chapter by outlining remaining challenges for implementing scalable and sustainable program interventions that aim to improve success rates for underrepresented men of Color.

Social Realities for Black Men in the United States

Any discussion about Black men in the United States must begin with observations about their economic and sociocultural position in our larger society. Although many view the election of a Black male president as a signifier for a postracial era, evidence suggests otherwise. For example, as of April 2015, the unemployment rate stands at 9% for Black men compared to just over 4% for White men (Bureau of Labor Statistics, 2015). Hamilton, Austin, and Darity (2011) report similar disparities when examining median income levels. Even when holding degree attainment constant across racial/ethnic categories, Black men earn 71% less than their White male counterparts. Black men are also disproportionate victims of the rising prison industrial complex in the United States. According to the Pew Research Center (2013), Black men are six times more likely than White men to be incarcerated. To place this trend in historical context, between 1960 and 2010, the incarceration rate for Black men tripled, making them more likely to be incarcerated than any other demographic group. Recent high-profile incidents of unarmed Black men killed during confrontations with law enforcement have sparked civil protests in several cities and public outrage.

Considering the alarming economic statistics alongside sociocultural realities for Black men provides a much-needed context for community college leaders attempting to remedy or correct educational inequity. Despite persistent systematic inequity, Black men are routinely framed as individuals with problems, individuals who have cultural deficiencies, and individuals who lack the motivation and determination to succeed. As such, emphasizing micro-level processes when focusing on reducing disparities for Black men allows intergenerational reproduction of structural oppression to flourish. Meritocratic ideologies further propagate focus on Black men rather than larger systemic inertia that has positioned them in disadvantageous ways—emphasis on getting Black men on "the right track" rather than a focus on the track itself. It is critical for community college practices to challenge these narratives rather than supporting them as institutional norms.

Common Practices Related to Men of Color at Community Colleges

Given the framing of disparities for men of Color as products of individual dispositions rather than outcomes of structural inequalities, it is not surprising that psychological paradigms shape programmatic efforts for this underserved population (Kaufman & Feldman, 2004; Kezar, 2011; Wood, Palmer, & Harris, 2015). Policy makers and administrators in higher education tend to focus on repositioning the "unmotivated" Black men closer to dominant forms of cultural capital (e.g., emphasis on individualism and competition) with little acknowledgement of structural practices that shape disparities. Employing this perspective is particularly troublesome at community colleges given the role these institutions serve as postsecondary entry point for Black men. As a primary path of access for this traditionally underserved population in higher education, it is critical for community colleges to adhere to their historical function as a gateway to postsecondary success for traditionally marginalized populations in higher education (Bragg, 2001; Dowd, 2007). Furthermore, as an individual focus tends to accentuate quantifiable measures of success, opportunities to reduce systematic origins of inequality for Black men attending community colleges are missed.

In their comprehensive review of published scholarship over the last 15 years on men of Color attending community colleges, Harris and Wood (2013) confirm the focus on individual agency in research and practice. Examinations of factors that influence student success of men of Color[3] tend to focus on integration (academic and social), individual dispositions toward environments (campus and community), and affective responses to campus contexts (formal and informal). Integrative factors include engagement with supportive faculty members and interactions with student peers. Individual dispositions include rejection of capitalistic values and embracing behaviors that reify stereotypical notions of men of Color. Affective variables are reflected by strong sense of belonging at the institution and construction of intersectional identities. Each set of domains encourages institutions to focus on micro-level dynamics when addressing disparate outcomes among men of Color attending community colleges.

Part of the issue, as Harris and Wood (2013) note, is that social integrationist perspectives primarily inform research on men of Color in community colleges. Integrationalist frameworks, such as Vincent Tinto's model of student departure, exemplify the practice of treating socially produced outcomes and patterns as rooted in individual actions (Kaufman & Feldman, 2004). As critics note in labeling college departure as a value-neutral action, assimilation frameworks often fail to acknowledge the unique social position and related experiences, both prior and during enrollment, for men of Color. Elaborating this point, Rendon, Jalomo, and Nora (2000) state, "Absent from the traditional social integrationist view are the distinctions among cultures, differences among students with regard to class, race, gender, and sexual orientation, and the role of group members and the institutions in assisting students to succeed" (p. 139). Indeed, Harris and Wood (2013) conclude their literature review with a call for implementation of policies and programs that center the role institutions play in the success or failure of men of Color attending community colleges.

Unfortunately, many community colleges fall short in addressing institutional conditions that disproportionately shape academic and social experiences of Black men on campus. If programming does exist for Black men, they are often the result of passionate efforts from individual faculty/administrators or located in a specialized student services office. In either situation, the opportunity to influence larger institutional norms is limited. Similarly, a significant limitation of contemporary community college research is the lack of qualitative research in examining institutional approaches toward addressing norms and practices that disproportionally influence experiences of Black men on campus. As Harris and Wood (2013) note, "Most of the published research on MOC in community colleges has been conducted from the quantitative research tradition. ... Qualitative research can illuminate how MOC experience community colleges, why notable trends and outcome inequities persist, and what meanings these students derive from their experience" (p. 182). To address limitations in policy, practice, and research, we offer the Together We Achieve (TWA) program at Parkland College as an illustrative example of an institutional approach toward equity for Black men attending community colleges.

Together We Achieve: An Institutional Approach to Equity for Men of Color

Parkland College is a midsize, public community college that offers associate degrees, certificates, continuing education opportunities, and specialized training to over 250,000 residents in 12 counties of East Central Illinois. Located in close proximity to the University of Illinois, students of Color account for approximately 30% of the student body, including 18% Black. In fall 2014, the second author of this chapter collected qualitative data on TWA, including faculty perspectives on the development of program and the experiences of students who recently completed or were completing participation.

Development of TWA. Dowd (2003) suggests that examination of detailed student outcome data is critical to developing equity-inclusive performance accountability measures. She states, "Equity-inclusive performance accountability calls for the use of outcome indicators to take an ideological turn away from valuing efficiency as a hallmark of good business practices to valuing efficiency as means to achieving outcome equity in higher education" (p. 24). Similarly, Parkland College used disaggregated institutional data to identify and address outcome inequalities among Black men entering the institution. The roots of the TWA can be traced to 2010 when the president of Parkland College, in response to rising developmental education needs among entering students, established an Innovation Fund to financially support the creation of a new system of developmental and college preparation at the institution. Among the innovations was the establishment of learning communities, where students enroll in the same set of courses and are supported by an adviser, mentor, and tutor. The intent of first-year learning communities at Parkland is to create an academic environment where college students focus on academic achievement, community building, and leadership development. All learning communities have similar goals: to create strong networking and bonding among students to foster peer-centered systems of success, to enhance support for students through social activities and advising, to produce opportunities for teamwork and collaborative learning, and to guide students to explore career options during the first year of college (Parkland College Office of Institutional Accountability and Research, 2014).

Informed by institutional data that revealed a disproportionate number of Black men in developmental education, as well as scholarship on Black men in higher education, administrators decided to create a specific learning community for Black men attending Parkland—Together We Achieve (TWA). The program included connecting students with faculty mentors who are committed to student learning and success. Additionally, students had access to academic advisors to discuss the multiple barriers that affected their academic progress. Tutoring was offered to students through the two semesters with trained professional tutors and learning assistance

New Directions for Community Colleges • DOI: 10.1002/cc

specialists. Finally, students were awarded scholarships for academic achievement in the learning community. To be eligible for enrollment in the TWA learning community, participants were required to be first-time, full-time students in the entering fall semester and in need of developmental education.

The first TWA learning community began at Parkland College in fall 2011 with 17 Black men. For the initial cohort, Parkland College's dean of academic services first attempted to recruit all Black men entering Parkland in fall 2011. However, the initial recruitment campaign netted very few interested applicants. Parkland administrators focused recruitment of Black men through the college's tutoring center, targeting students based on their ACT COMPASS placement scores and enrollment in developmental reading and writing in the fall 2011 semester. The TWA learning community curricular structure included enrolling all participants in at least two developmental education courses (English, math, or reading), at least one general education course (e.g., political science), and one college-planning course (Success in College). By situating developmental education as one of many curricular components of the learning community, administrators aimed to reduce stigmas associated with remedial education programs, particularly for underrepresented populations (Colyar, 2011; Levin & Calcagno, 2008).

Identifying increased placement in developmental education among incoming students, especially Black men, senior administrative leaders took a proactive approach toward redeveloping institutional practices. Rather than attribute academic disparities exclusively to individual choices, practitioners at Parkland emphasized a shift in institutional norms for academic services related to developmental education by creating a learning community. Prioritizing a learning community specifically focused on Black men signaled to campus and external communities that outcome equity for this population is a core metric for evaluating the overall success of the institution. Emphasizing a learning community for Black males served as a response to outcome disparities for that population at the institutions with a secondary focus on Black men who initially tested into developmental education courses.

From Validation to Community Building.   The theory of student validation, an asset-based approach to student retention and persistence in postsecondary education, supports key components of TWA. Rendon (1994) theorizes that active intervention in the form of validation encourages nontraditional students to gain a sense of belonging in the academic environment and enhances their self-efficacy, also referred to as self-confidence (Bandura, 1997). Validation is defined as a supportive and confirming process initiated by validating institutional agents (mentors, faculty, professionals, peers) that fosters academic and interpersonal development. The validation framework offers two forms of validation—academic and interpersonal (Linares & Muñoz, 2011; Rendon, 1994). Academic validation represents supportive actions that foster academic development.

New Directions for Community Colleges • DOI: 10.1002/cc

Examples include learning opportunities that empower students, meaningful feedback on academic work, and individualized tutorial attention. Interpersonal validation represents actions that support personal and social adjustment to institutional settings. This includes encouraging involvement in campus events and informal conversations with institutional agents (particularly faculty).

TWA participants shared experiences of interactions with faculty, both inside and outside of the classroom, that fostered both academic and interpersonal forms of validation. They describe willingness of TWA faculty to provide academic support and personal mentoring to assist TWA students in their academic endeavors. A student notes:

> My biggest supporter, besides my friends in TWA, is (Developmental Writing professor). … [She] showed me that it was important to learn these subjects and that I was also an important part of the TWA learning community. Because of her helping me build my confidence, I now speak out in my other classes.

Further, faculty members designed small-group discussions in the TWA classes, arranged off-campus social events, and were available for formal and casual mentoring sessions. TWA participants showed deep appreciation to faculty for the extra time, describing it as a valuable component to their identity development as a college. As one student mentions,

> I mean here is a teacher who doesn't really need to spend time with us outside of class … he's got a wife and kids and all. … It felt good. It felt like I was a part of something special. … I mean I felt like this was my college, and I was a part of it.

As Castro (Chapter 1) reminds us, the primary goal of equity-oriented practices in education is to provide resources for students, particularly those from traditionally underserved populations, to reach their full potential. A critical step toward this goal is to validate student beliefs about their capabilities as a valuable partner in the learning process. This process cannot happen if educators subscribe to deficit-thinking perspectives of students. Rather, it acknowledges that many students enter postsecondary education with damaging experiences that have unfairly eroded academic self-confidence. As participants in TWA demonstrate, when the validating process elevates levels of self-efficacy among underserved populations, students can begin to move toward the center of community development (academic and social) at the institution.

Toward a Collective Agency Among Black Men at Parkland.   In considering persistence as a form of individual agency, research in higher education tends to emphasize micro-level access to traditional forms of social and cultural capital (Winkle-Wagner, 2010). In contrast, Yosso

(2005) offers a framework, cultural community wealth, which centers on collectivist perspectives. Cultural community wealth refers to knowledge, skills, and abilities possessed and used by Communities of Color to successfully survive at Predominately White Institutions (PWIs). Among the forms of community wealth is familial capital. "This form of cultural wealth engages a commitment to community well-being and expands the concept of family to include a more broad understanding of kinship" (p. 79).

Perspectives from TWA students on their experiences in the program highlight the value of and reliance on familial capital in shaping institutional experiences. A common view that surfaced through the observations and interviews with TWA students was that a shared commitment or engagement helped keep TWA intact and was the central ingredient in how successful the learning community format was for improving academic levels of these Black men. The primary goal of TWA when it was designed was, in the words of Dr. Hightower, Parkland dean of academic services and director of TWA, "to serve as a bridge to college coursework" but in constructing this metaphorical bridge to "success" the TWA administrative leaders, faculty, and senior administration began to see visible outcomes related to investment in the learning community. With access to a positive environment at the institution, a group that is often labeled as "oppositional" to education succeeded. This had a powerful influence not only on the members of the TWA learning community but also on other Black men at the college. One student, Marcus, explained how he felt about TWA:

> You know TWA is place where we can help each other out, like last semester when we were all hurting in (Parkland faculty) math class so we started getting together in (study room in the Academic Success Center) and then after that we just studied together all the time. I think we all passed Math 070 … brothers helping brothers.

Whereas Marcus's story talked about interaction through studying together, Larry expounded on Marcus's experience and shared what he felt was a sense of community and belongingness he received from the peer relationships forged in the TWA learning cohort:

> I feel culturally connected to the TWA program because it has been made for us. It is designed to relate to our own experiences and give value to them. I like that a lot about TWA. Yeah, we are young Black dudes and we are not here to make trouble like everybody thinks we are. We are here to learn just like the rest of students. Our experiences are valuable and help us to learn this stuff (referring the college courses). It is a beautiful thing. If you want my honest opinion … I wish more brothers in the program and outside of it could see what kind of opportunity this is for them. Parkland wants to better our situation. You got to have courage if you want to stay in school. It is hard work … hardest thing I've ever done, but man it is worth it.

Contrary to the perception that Black men tend to prefer a hyper-masculine, competitive "cool-pose" stance toward education, evidence from participants of TWA suggests an inclination toward collectivist experiences supported by familial capital. This observation supports previous research that finds communal bonds among males of Color as critical to heightening individual perceptions of supportive structures (Baber, 2014). As connections among Black men (and between Black men and faculty/administrators) are developed through trust and reciprocity, individualism gives way to a form of collective agency. Through this process, knowledge about academic and social practices at Parkland is equitably distributed (e.g., "brothers helping brothers") rather than individually accumulated. Furthermore, the criteria for success are not isolated to personal accomplishment but viewed as an interdependent, collective outcome.

Conclusion

In addition to observations of affective and behavioral patterns, preliminary data reveal that Black men participating in Together We Achieve successfully complete the developmental education sequence at a significantly higher rate than Black men who are not enrolled in the TWA learning community (57% versus 21%). Although development of TWA reflects a starting point for equity leadership at Parkland—acknowledgement of outcome disparities and prioritizing programs to address these issues—several challenges remain. Parkland will be challenged in supporting scalability efforts to reach more Black men entering campus (and developing similar programs for other underrepresented men of Color), particularly if economic and administrative resources remain stagnant. Sustainability beyond the grant funding period and current tenure of senior leadership will also be critical in making TWA practices a permanent part of institutional norms toward Black men attending the institution. One potential solution for scalability and sustainability is partnering with external constituencies (e.g., local businesses, high school partners, and community activists) to ensure that Together We Achieve is part of a larger institutional effort toward providing transformative educational opportunities for Black men in the district. Based on workforce development goals, local businesses may be interested in providing supplemental financial support for programs like TWA. Similarly, high schools may consider collaborating with Parkland, viewing TWA as a resource for promoting college readiness among Black men in the secondary school system. Community activists may also view TWA as a valuable asset for addressing gaps in education, employment, and health outcomes for Black men in the community.

As these collaborative efforts develop around programs such as TWA, it will be critical to address the interest-convergence dilemma that often steers equity programs away from social justice foundations and toward a neoliberal rationale (Baber, 2015). Interest-convergence stresses that social change benefitting traditionally marginalized populations occurs only when it converges with the best interests of the dominant political elite (Bell, 1980, 2003). Left unchecked, convergence of interests around institutional programs for Black men attending community colleges is likely to move programmatic goals toward the direction of neoliberal interests, emphasizing success based solely on economic outcomes (e.g., development of human capital). Although such dilemmas may be largely unavoidable for community college administrators in the current sociopolitical environment, the importance of acknowledging the potential influence of neoliberal interests on programs such as TWA cannot be overstated. This requires community college practitioners to consciously center (and recenter as necessary) concepts of equity as part of sustainable and scalable efforts for improving structural conditions for Black men on campus.

Despite increasing attention toward Black men in higher education over the last decade, persistent outcome disparities suggest that additional efforts are required. As a significant point entry into the postsecondary system for Black men, community colleges may serve as a valuable vehicle for providing supportive climate for this traditionally marginalized student population. An institutional approach, as exemplified in this chapter by Together We Achieve at Parkland College in Champaign, Illinois, has potential to provide support for holistic development and long-term success among Black men on campus.

Notes

1. Although we focus on Black men in this chapter, we acknowledge similar disparities among other men of Color—specifically, Latinos, Native Americans, Alaskan Natives/Pacific Islanders, and Asian Americans. We encourage scholars to continue to build scholarship centering the experiences of all men of Color student populations.

2. In this chapter, we privilege the term Black as a descriptor of socially constructed racial/ethnic categories as they reflect the sociocultural heterogeneity within the Black diaspora (e.g., Caribbean/African).

3. Harris and Wood (2013) note the majority of these studies focus on Black men.

References

Baber, L. D. (2014). When aspiration meets opportunity: Examining transitional experiences of African American males in college readiness programs. *Community College Journal of Research and Practice, 38*(12), 1097–1111.

Baber, L. D. (2015). Considering the interest-convergence dilemma in STEM education. *The Review of Higher Education, 38*(2), 251–270.

Bandura, A. (1997). *Self-efficacy: The exercise of control.* New York, NY: Freeman.

Bell, D. A. (1980). *Brown v. Board of Education* and the interest-convergence dilemma. *Harvard Law Review, 93*(3), 518–533.

Bell, D. A. (2003). Diversity's distractions. *Columbia Law Review, 103,* 1622–1633.

Bragg, D. D. (2001). Community college access, mission, and outcomes: Considering intriguing intersections and challenges. *Peabody Journal of Education, 76*(1), 93–116.

Bureau of Labor Statistics. (2015). *Table A2: Employment status of the civilian population by race, sex, and age.* Retrieved from http://www.bls.gov/news.release/empsit.t02.htm

Colyar, J. (2011). Strangers in a strange land. In A. Kezar (Ed.), *Recognizing and serving low-income students in higher education* (pp. 121–138). New York, NY: Routledge.

Dowd, A. C. (2003). From access to outcome equity: Revitalizing the democratic mission of the community college. *Annals of the American Academy, 585,* 1–28.

Dowd, A. C. (2007). Community colleges as gateways and gatekeepers: Moving beyond the access "saga" toward outcome equity. *Harvard Educational Review, 77*(4), 407–419.

Hamilton, D., Austin, A., & Darity, W. (2011). *Whiter jobs, higher wages: Occupational segregation and the lower wages of Black men* (Briefing Paper #288). Washington, DC: Economic Policy Institute.

Harris, F., III, & Wood, J. L. (2013). Student success for men of color in community colleges: A review of published literature and research, 1998–2012. *Journal of Diversity in Higher Education, 6*(3), 174–185.

Kaufman, P., & Feldman, K. A. (2004). Forming identities in college: A sociological approach. *Research in Higher Education, 45*(5), 463–496.

Kezar, A. (Ed.). (2011). *Recognizing and serving low-income students in higher education.* New York, NY: Routledge.

Levin, H. M., & Calcagno, J. C. (2008). Remediation in the community college: An evaluator's perspective. *Community College Review, 35*(3), 181–207.

Linares, L. I. R., & Muñoz, S. M. (2011). Revisiting validation theory: Theoretical foundations, applications, and extensions. *Enrollment Management Journal, 2*(1), 12–33.

National Center for Education Statistics. (2012). *Higher education: Gaps in access and persistence study* (NCES 2012-046). Washington, DC: U.S. Department of Education.

National Center for Education Statistics. (2014). *Table 302.60.* Retrieved from http://nces.ed.gov/programs/digest/d13/tables/dt13_302.60.asp

Parkland College Office of Institutional Accountability and Research. (2014). *Data report on Together We Achieve learning community.* Champaign, IL: Parkland College.

Pew Research Center. (2013). *Incarceration gap between Whites and Blacks widens.* Retrieved from http://www.pewresearch.org/fact-tank/2013/09/06/incarceration-gap-between-whites-and-blacks-widens/

Rendon, L. I. (1994). Validating culturally diverse students: Toward a new model of learning and student development. *Innovative Higher Education, 19*(1), 33–51.

Rendon, L. I., Jalomo, R. E., & Nora, A. (2000). Theoretical considerations in the study of minority student retention in higher education. In J. M. Braxton (Ed.), *Reworking the student departure puzzle* (pp. 127–156). Nashville, TN: Vanderbilt University Press.

Winkle-Wagner, R. (2010). *Cultural capital: The uses and abuses of a key theoretical concept in educational research* (ASHE Higher Education Report Series, Vol. 36, No. 1). San Francisco, CA: Jossey-Bass.

Wood, J. L., Palmer, R. T., & Harris, F., III. (2015). Men of color in community colleges: A synthesis of empirical findings. In M. B. Paulson & J. C. Smart (Eds.), *Higher education: Handbook of theory and research* (pp. 431–468). Dordrecht, The Netherlands: Springer International Publishing.

Yosso, T. J. (2005). Whose culture has capital? A critical race theory discussion of community cultural wealth. *Race Ethnicity and Education, 8,* 69–91.

LORENZO BABER, PHD, *is an associate professor of higher education and community college leadership at Iowa State University.*

RANDY FLETCHER, PHD, *is dean for career and transfer at Parkland College.*

EDMUND GRAHAM, MED, *is a doctoral candidate in education policy, organization and leadership at the University of Illinois, Urbana-Champaign.*

INDEX

Ackerman, R., 79
ADN program. *See* Associate degree nursing (ADN) program
Ahern, A., 77, 86
Alcantar, C., 90
American Graduates Initiative, 17
Argyris, C., 28, 35, 46
Associate degree nursing (ADN) program, 46–53
Austin, A., 98

Baber, L. D., 97, 105, 107
Baime, D., 67, 68
Bandura, A., 102
Barber, E. G., 22
Bathmaker, A., 44
Bauman, G. L., 28
Bell, D. A., 106
Bensimon, E. M., 5, 25, 27–29, 31, 33, 34, 38, 40, 42
Bettinger, E. P., 68
Bishop, R., 39
Black men, at community colleges: overview, 97–98; social realities in United States, 98–99; "unmotivated," 99. *See also* Men of Color (MOC)
Blumenfeld, W. J., 60–62
Bragg, D. D., 43, 44, 55, 99
Bryan, C. J., 79
Burnett, S. E., 79

Calcagno, J. C., 102
Campbell, C. A., 67, 76
Carnevale, A. P., 19, 20
Castañeda, C., 22
Castro, E. L., 1, 4, 5, 9, 13
CCA. *See* Community College of Aurora (CCA)
Center for Urban Education (CUE), 25–26
Chaparro, G., 87, 96
Chavez, M. L., 92
Chen, A. C. R., 87
Chong, F., 44
Choudhuri, D. D., 60
Church, T. E., 78, 79
Cole, S., 22

Collaborative learning, in Equity Scorecard, 28
College presidents, role of, 18, 21–23
Colyar, J., 102
Community College of Aurora (CCA), 25, 32, 35, 40
Coronado, H., 94
Cortés, R., 94, 95
Cray, A., 59
CUE. *See* Center for Urban Education (CUE)

Darity, W., 98
D'Augelli, A., 60
Deil-Amen, R., 67, 76
Denning, S., 46
Dewey, J., 27
DiRamio, D., 77, 79
Disabled veteran outreach placement specialist (DVOP), 83
Double-loop learning, in Equity Scorecard, 28
Dowd, A. C., 5, 29, 31, 38, 40, 99, 101
Dozier, S. B., 88
Dresser, L., 44
DVOP. *See* Disabled veteran outreach placement specialist (DVOP)

Equity-minded learning, in Equity Scorecard, 28
Equity-mindedness, 31, 38–40
Equity Scorecard: African-American equity gaps and goals from, 33, 34; aspects of learning in, 28; collaborative learning in, 28; diversity workers team, 30; double-loop learning in, 28; equity-minded learning in, 28; framework of, 27; Hispanic/Latino equity gaps and goals from, 34; impact of, 40–41; inequalities in educational outcomes and, 27–28; overview, 25–26; phases of, 28–37; "Syllabus Review" protocol, 30
Equity work: challenges in performing, 8–10; concept of, 6–8; diversity and, 15–24; overview, 5–6; relearning and, 10–12

FAFSA. *See* Free Application for Federal Student Aid (FAFSA)

Feldman, K. A., 99, 100

Felix, E. R., 25, 42

Fette, R., 60

Financial aid: better data collection for, 74; delays in disbursement of, 70–71; flexible disbursement of, 74–75; information dissemination, 74; overview, 67–68; procedural and eligibility issues for, 71–73; recommendations for action, 73–75; student's experience, 69–73; subsidies in, 73–74

Fletcher, R., 97, 107

Foster, M., 77, 86

Franklin, K., 60

Frazer, S., 60–62

Free Application for Federal Student Aid (FAFSA), 67, 68, 73

Garvey, J., 60, 62

Garza Mitchell, R. L., 79

Gay, Lesbian, & Straight Education Network (GLSEN), 63

Geller, W. W., 60

Glider, P., 60

GLSEN. *See* Gay, Lesbian, & Straight Education Network (GLSEN)

Goldrick-Rab, S., 74

Goulding, J., 79

GPA. *See* Grade point average (GPA)

Grade point average (GPA), 72–73

Graham, E., 97, 107

Gray, J., 25, 42

Guarneros, N., 90

Guided inquiry, 37–38

Gutierrez, M., 22

Hamilton, D., 98

Hamrick, F. A., 79

Hanson, D., 25, 42

Harmon, T., 45

Harris, F., 99, 100

Harris, F., III., 97, 99

Hatzenbuehler, M. I., 59

Head, D., 77, 86

Herek, G. M., 59

Heterosexism, 59–60

Homophobia, 59

Hope, D., 60

Hurtado, S., 10

Institutional Undocu-Competence (IUC), 87–95; college outreach and recruitment for, 91–92; overview, 87–88; training college faculty and staff, 89–90; for visible and open advocacy, 90–91

Integrated Postsecondary Education Data System (IPEDS), 32

IPEDS. *See* Integrated Postsecondary Education Data System (IPEDS)

IUC. *See* Institutional Undocu-Competence (IUC)

Jalomo, R. E., 100

Jauregui, J. A., 91

Kanter, M., 44

Katsinas, S. G., 22

Kaufman, P., 99, 100

Kemmis, S., 25

Kendall, N., 73

Kezar, A., 98, 99

Kisch, J., 60

Klingsmith., L., 25, 42

Krieger, S. L., 63

Kumagai, A. K., 87

LACCD. *See* Los Angeles Community College District (LACCD)

Leadership: LGBTQ students and, 63; requirement of, 19–20; role of, 18

Leider, S. J., 60

Leino, E. V., 60

Lesbian, gay, bisexual, transgender, and queer (LGBTQ) students, 57–64; campus resources and policies for, 63–64; climate survey and needs assessment for, 61–62; faculty and staff training and development for, 62–63; heterosexism and, 59–60; homophobia and, 59; inclusivity in community colleges, 61–64; institutional commitment to support, 61; overview, 57–58; peer outreach and leadership, 63; social and policy context, 58–60

Levin, H. M., 102

LGBTQ culture, 57–64

LGBTQ students. *See* Lesbian, gay, bisexual, transgender, and queer (LGBTQ) students

Linares, L. I. R., 102

Liss, L., 45
Long, B. T., 68, 73
Lorenz, G. L., 29
Los Angeles Community College District (LACCD), 15
Lypson, M. L., 87

Malaney, G. D., 60
Malcolm, Z., 68
Malcom, L. E., 25, 29
Malcom-Piqueux, L. E., 40
Manning, P., 60
McKinney, L., 68
McTaggart, R., 25
Meidlinger, P. C., 60
Mendez, J. P., 68
Mendoza, P., 68
Men of Color (MOC): institutional approach to equity for, 101–105; overview, 97–98; practices related to, 99–100; TWA program for, 98, 101–105. See also Black men, at community colleges
Military Times, 78
Mitchell, R. L., 79
Montiel, G. I., 87, 96
Moon, T. L., 79
Morest, V., 53
Mullin, C., 67, 68
Muñoz, S. M., 90, 102

Nakamoto, J., 29
Nassif, R., 44
Nelson, C. D., 60
Nelson, E. S., 63
Neumann, A., 29
New York Times, 18
Nora, A., 100
Novak, H., 68

Obergefell vs. Hodges, 59
OCCRL. See Office of Community College Research and Leadership (OCCRL)
Ochoa, E., 44
Office of Community College Research and Leadership (OCCRL), 43
Oliverez, P., 92
Oreopoulos, P., 68

Palmer, R. T., 97, 99
Pathways to Results (PTR), 43–54; ADN program and, 46–53; equity and outcomes assessment, 45; implementation in Illinois, 46–50; lessons learned in, 52–54; methods, 44–46; overview, 43–44; process assessment, 45; program improvement and evaluation, 46; review and reflection, 46; solutions from, 50–52
Patton, M., 43
Perez, I., 87, 96
Pérez, W., 87, 90, 91, 94–96
Pickel, J., 43, 55
Pollock, M., 26
Pring, L., 60

Radford, A. W., 77
Ramos, K., 94
Rankin, S., 60–62
Rendon, L. I., 100, 102
Rhoads, R. A., 60
Rios-Aguilar, C., 67, 76
Rodriguez, F. C., 15, 24
Rose, M., 60
Roy, A., 10
Rudd, M. D., 79
Ruiz, A., 10
Rumann, C. B., 79

Salt Lake Community College (SLCC), 78
Sanbonmatsu, L., 68
SAP. See Satisfactory Academic Progress (SAP)
Satisfactory Academic Progress (SAP), 72
Schma, G. A., 79
Schön, D. A., 28, 35
Schools App, 68–69
Segoria, J., 79
Shackelford, A. L., 79
Shelton, E. N., 51
Shepard, N., 73
Silverman, M. M., 60
Slate, J. R., 91
SLCC. See Salt Lake Community College (SLCC)
SLCC veterans center, development of: community collaboration, 83; Disability Resource Center (DRC), 82; disability resource services and, 81–82; partnership with Department of Veterans Affairs, 82–83; social support, 81
SLCC veterans' services: addressing challenges to student veteran

community, 79–80; development of center, 80–83. *See also* SLCC veterans' center, development of; increasing accessibility of, 79–80; overview, 77–79; recommendations for, 83–84; suggestions for, 79

Smith-Osborne, A., 79

Smith, W., 44

Soriano, M., 92

Stallone Brown, M., 91

Stripling, J., 57

Strohl, J., 19

Taylor, J. L., 57, 60, 62, 66

Tetreault, P. A., 60

Together We Achieve (TWA) program, 98, 101–105; development of, 101–102; from validation to community building, 102–103

TWA program. *See* Together We Achieve (TWA) program

Umbricht, M., 45

Undocumented students, 87–95; as equity issue, 88; financial aid for, 92–93; health and psychological services for, 93–94; institutional support for, 93; policy and assessment recommendations for, 88–89

Valencia, R., 9

Valenzuela, J. I., 87, 96

Veterans Integration to Academic Leadership (VITAL), 82–83

VetSuccess On Campus (VSOC), 82

VITAL. *See* Veterans Integration to Academic Leadership (VITAL)

VSOC. *See* VetSuccess On Campus (VSOC)

Washington Higher Education Secretariat (WHES), 18

Weber, G. N., 60–62

Wenger, E., 28

Western Interstate Commission of Higher Education (WICHE), 25

Wheelahan, L., 44

WHES. *See* Washington Higher Education Secretariat (WHES)

WICHE. *See* Western Interstate Commission of Higher Education (WICHE)

Williams, E. A., 60

Williams, M., 51

Witham, K., 40

Wood, J. L., 97, 99, 100

Zamani-Gallaher, E. M., 60

CC171 Community College Faculty Scholarship
John M. Braxton
While teaching occupies the primary role of faculty members in community colleges, the question remains: To what extent are community college faculty members engaged in research and scholarship? This issue of *New Directions for Community Colleges* focuses on:

- the types of research and scholarship performed by community college faculty,
- the forces that foster or impede the engagement of community college faculty members in research and scholarship,
- specific examples of community college faculty scholarship that demonstrate the value of this work to the institution and to larger society, and
- policies and practices at the institutional, local, and state level that support engagement in research and scholarship.

This volume will be of interest to public policy makers, members of governing boards of community colleges, presidents, and chief academic affairs officers of community colleges, as well as scholars, faculty members, and graduate students in higher education programs.
ISBN: 978-1-119-13328-5

CC170 Bringing College Education Into Prisons
Robert Scott
This sourcebook on "Bringing College Education Into Prisons" is addressed to community college educators who are interested in the over two million people incarcerated in the United States today. It introduces the basic concept of college in prison, describes programs that exist across the country today, and considers the challenges and opportunities facing community college educators who are interested in the growing movement to reintroduce postsecondary education to America's prisons. Not only do the authors write from their personal experience as educators, they also expound on many issues that arise in prison teaching, including:

- the clash between college assumptions and prison rules,
- the complete absence of public funding for college in prison,
- the racial dimension of mass incarceration, and
- insights on key issues facing college educators in the prison context today.

Community college educators, academic and policy leaders are called upon to contribute to the growing movement to make community college education available to incarcerated adults as part of a wider societal shift away from mass incarceration, and toward a more just and peaceful society.
ISBN: 978-11191-07156

CC169 Dual Enrollment Policies, Pathways, and Perspectives
Jason L. Taylor, Joshua Pretlow
Dual enrollment is an expanding program that allows high school students to accrue college credits prior to high school graduation. Advocates of dual enrollment point to the financial and academic benefits of dual enrollment, and accumulating research suggests dual enrollment has a positive impact on students' access to and success in college. In this volume of *New Directions for Community Colleges*, aspects of dual enrollment practices and policies will be explained, including:

- state policies that regulate dual enrollment practice and the influence of state policy on local practice,
- the usage of dual enrollment programs as a pathway for different populations of students such as career and technical education students and students historically underrepresented in higher education, and
- chapters that surface student, faculty, and high school stakeholder perspectives and that examine institutional and partnership performance and quality.

This volume addresses issues and topics critical for community college leaders, administrators, and policymakers to engage in and understand as they develop new dual enrollment programs or adapt and revamp existing dual enrollment programs.
ISBN: 978-11190-54184

CC168 Budget and Finance in the American Community College
Trudy H. Bers, Ronald B. Head, James C. Palmer
The literature about budgets and finance in community colleges is surprisingly sparse and most is dated. In this volume of *New Directions for Community Colleges*, key issues and practices will be addressed on the following topics:

- the contemporary challenge of meeting growing demands for increased student persistence and success,
- diminishing state support for higher education,
- new calls for accountability and ways to measure institutional effectiveness,
- the increasing reliance of many community colleges on grants and other sources of revenue, and
- college policies that have significant financial ramifications.

The intended audience for this volume includes community college leaders, new administrators, board members, budget and finance staff, and faculty and students in higher education and community college graduate programs. The volume may also be a useful overview for budget and finance leaders such as chief financial officers.
ISBN: 978-11190-41566

NEW DIRECTIONS FOR COMMUNITY COLLEGE
ORDER FORM SUBSCRIPTION AND SINGLE ISSUES

DISCOUNTED BACK ISSUES:

Use this form to receive 20% off all back issues of *New Directions for Community College*.
All single issues priced at **$23.20** (normally $29.00)

TITLE	ISSUE NO.	ISBN

Call 1-800-835-6770 or see mailing instructions below. When calling, mention the promotional code JBNND to receive your discount. For a complete list of issues, please visit www.wiley.com/WileyCDA/WileyTitle/productCd-CC.html

SUBSCRIPTIONS: (1 YEAR, 4 ISSUES)

☐ New Order   ☐ Renewal

U.S.	☐ Individual: $89	☐ Institutional: $356
CANADA/MEXICO	☐ Individual: $89	☐ Institutional: $398
ALL OTHERS	☐ Individual: $113	☐ Institutional: $434

Call 1-800-835-6770 or see mailing and pricing instructions below.
Online subscriptions are available at www.onlinelibrary.wiley.com

ORDER TOTALS:

Issue / Subscription Amount: $ _____

Shipping Amount: $ _____
(for single issues only – subscription prices include shipping)

Total Amount: $ _____

SHIPPING CHARGES:	
First Item	$6.00
Each Add'l Item	$2.00

(No sales tax for U.S. subscriptions. Canadian residents, add GST for subscription orders. Individual rate subscriptions must be paid by personal check or credit card. Individual rate subscriptions may not be resold as library copies.)

BILLING & SHIPPING INFORMATION:

☐ **PAYMENT ENCLOSED:** *(U.S. check or money order only. All payments must be in U.S. dollars.)*

☐ **CREDIT CARD:**   ☐ VISA   ☐ MC   ☐ AMEX

Card number _____ Exp. Date _____

Card Holder Name _____ Card Issue # _____

Signature _____ Day Phone _____

☐ **BILL ME:** *(U.S. institutional orders only. Purchase order required.)*

Purchase order # _____
          Federal Tax ID 13559302 • GST 89102-8052

Name _____

Address _____

Phone _____ E-mail _____

Copy or detach page and send to: **John Wiley & Sons, Inc. / Jossey Bass**
                    PO Box 55381
                    Boston, MA 02205-9850

PROMO JBNND